Measurement and Recording of Historic Buildings

Measurement and Recording of Historic Buildings

PETER SWALLOW
Professor of Building Surveying,
School of the Built Environment,
De Montfort University, Leicester

DAVID WATT
Assistant Conservation Officer,
Norfolk County Council

ROBERT ASHTON
Director Leicester CAD Centre,
School of the Built Environment,
De Montfort University, Leicester

DONHEAD

First published in the United Kingdom in 1993 by
Donhead Publishing
28 Southdean Gardens
Wimbledon
London SW19 6NU
Tel: 081-789 0138

ISBN 1 873394 08 X

A CIP catalogue record for this book is available from the
British Library.

Typeset by Keyboard Services, Luton
Printed in Great Britain at The Alden Press, Oxford

Contents

Preface

There are several types of survey relating to land and buildings which may be undertaken, and the following are just a few examples:

♦ Measured surveys of land to show topographical features, boundaries, buildings, roads and other development infrastructure.
♦ Valuation surveys of land and buildings for acquisition, compensation, disposal, investment, insurance, mortgage or rating purposes.
♦ Visual surveys of the structure and fabric of buildings to assess their condition and to prepare structural survey reports, schedules of condition, schedules of dilapidations, or specifications for programmes of maintenance and repair.
♦ Measured surveys of buildings to provide drawings of their layout, construction and appearance.

This book confines itself to measured surveys undertaken to enable accurate scaled drawings to be prepared of buildings and their immediate surroundings for any of the following purposes:

♦ To provide a physical record for legal purposes, for example deed and lease plans.
♦ To supply information about the construction and layout of buildings, together with their associated facilities and services, to assist property managers and others to utilize and maintain their physical assets efficiently.
♦ To form the base drawings for proposed programmes of work involving repairs, alterations, adaptations or extensions.
♦ To record the relationships of buildings to their sites, for example a country house to its formal garden and surrounding parkland.

♦ To record the plan, structure and chronological development of a building in order that its history might be interpreted and understood,
♦ To record historic built fabric before repairs, alterations or demolition lead to obliteration or complete loss.

The aim of this book is to provide a practical guide for those responsible for commissioning or executing measured surveys as a means of recording buildings and their associated sites. Starting with the basic principles of surveying, the reader is taken, step-by-step, to a level that will enable an accurate measured survey to be executed using traditional techniques and low-cost equipment. Later chapters deal with more recent developments in measured survey technique using sophisticated computing and surveying equipment. Whilst the procedures and techniques described here may be used to measure land and buildings of any description, because of a growing concern to protect and conserve our architectural heritage there is an emphasis on the recording of historic buildings and their settings.

The book is arranged with the main body of the text describing the processes and techniques employed in the preparation of a measured survey. Two distinct processes are identified: *surveying*, which involves measuring and recording the dimensions of land and buildings; and *computation and plotting*, a process which subsequently translates the survey sketches and notes into finished drawings.

In collecting measurements on site, and to enable plans, sections and elevations to be drawn up, the surveyor may use a number of techniques either singly or in combination. Those that are covered include:

♦ Annotated and dimensioned sketches.
♦ Hand measurement, using tapes and rods.
♦ Measurement using optical survey instruments such as level and staff, theodolite.
♦ Optoelectronic survey techniques using electromagnetic distance measuring (EDM) equipment, total station theodolites.
♦ Recording and storing survey data in the field electronically on portable computers.
♦ Photography.
♦ Rectified photography.
♦ Close-range stereo-photogrammetry.
♦ Computer-aided mono-photogrammetry.

In dealing with the production of finished survey drawings, both traditional draughting practice and computer-aided draughting techniques are covered.

The appendices show the practical application of the techniques described in the main text by reference to case study material drawn from a range of measured surveys.

Extensive use has been made of illustrations as an aid to understanding the essential principles of measuring and recording, and to help those new to the subject to conduct surveys and produce accurate drawings with confidence. The authors hope that readers, be they architects, builders, conservation officers, industrial archaeologists, planners or surveyors, will find the book of value.

The authors are grateful to Richard Hoile for preparing the line drawings and to the following individuals, organizations and practices that kindly agreed to allow their survey drawings and field-notes to be reproduced in the appendices: Bruce Bradley; Hilary Brightman; Denise Sweeney; Robert Smith; Norfolk County Council; John Severn of Severn Stewart; Architects, Nottingham; S. A. Wright, Architects, Coventry, and Derek Latham and Company, Architects, Derby. Additionally, we should like to thank the following for permission to reproduce photographs: Cloud 9 Photographic Services Limited, Sutton-on-Trent, Nottinghamshire (Figure 8.3); English Heritage Photogrammetric Unit, York (Figures 8.6 and 8.7); and Leicester CAD Centre (Figures 8.1, 8.2 and 8.8).

CHAPTER ONE

Basic Survey Practice

Surveying is the science principally concerned with the accurate measurement of the earth and its features, both natural and man-made. This book confines itself to that branch of surveying known as *plane surveying*. Plane surveying deals with the measurement of areas of land and their associated built infrastructure that are so limited in their extent that the area being surveyed is assumed to lie on a flat plane, and the curvature of the earth is ignored.

Whereas *surveying* is undertaken to determine relative positions in the horizontal plane, *levelling* is concerned with vertical measurements to determine the heights of features relative to a datum surface, such as sea level.

By combining surveying and levelling information a complete picture of the topography of a piece of land can be obtained and presented in the form of a map or, at a more detailed level, drawings produced to record buildings and civil engineering structures constructed on the land.

Before looking at the basic principles that underlie surveying practices and techniques, it is helpful to trace the development of the discipline.

HISTORICAL DEVELOPMENT OF SURVEYING

Surveying theory and instrumentation have evolved over many centuries, much of it developing from the practices of other academic disciplines, notably astronomy, geometry and navigation. The work of Euclid of Alexandria (*circa* 1000 BC) on geometry and arithmetic, in particular, had a profound effect on the theory and survey practices used in the Roman Empire.

The Roman land surveyors, or *agrimensores*, made use of simple pieces of equipment such as the *groma* (Figure 1.1). The groma consisted of a pole about 1200 mm high, on top of which a cross was laid flat. At each end of the cross were suspended weighted strings (plumb-bobs), which when hanging parallel to the central pole meant that it was perpendicular, so straight lines and right angles could be marked off by sighting down the intersecting arms of the cross. To determine a reliable horizontal datum line the Romans used a *chorobate*, or water level, which Vitruvius (*The Ten Books of Architecture*, Book VIII, Chapter V) describes as being a straightedge, some six metres in length supported on legs at each end (Figure 1.2). The chorobate was known to be level when plumb-lines fastened to the straightedge hung parallel to vertical lines marked on braces connecting the instrument with its legs. The setting up of the chorobate could be double-checked by pouring water into a groove worked into the top edge of the straightedge and seeing that it came uniformly up to the rim of the groove. By sighting along the levelled straightedge, Roman engineers, using measuring rods and lines, could measure the vertical distance between the line of sight and the ground at predetermined intervals to obtain the profile of the land being surveyed (Figure 1.3).

During the Middle Ages, surveyors continued to make only simple direct measurements. They used lines, rods or just pacing to determine length;

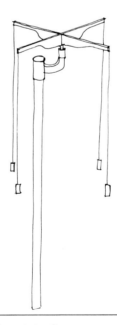

Figure 1.1   Groma.

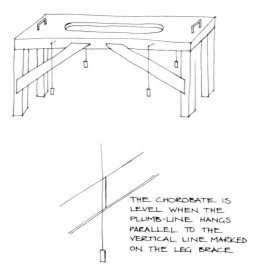

THE CHOROBATE IS
LEVEL WHEN THE
PLUMB-LINE HANGS
PARALLEL TO THE
VERTICAL LINE MARKED
ON THE LEG BRACE

Figure 1.2 Chorobate.

and the groma, plumb-line and water-level for setting out right angles and establishing horizontals and verticals.

Surveying instrumentation and practice advanced quickly during the sixteenth century. In 1512 the *potimetrum* was designed for taking bearings and altitudes, and also for levelling. In its construction it represented a prototype for the theodolite. A notable technical advance was made in 1533 when Gemma Frisius (1508–55) explained the principle of triangulation, which utilizes a framework of triangles in which all the angles and one side length are measured. The remaining sides are computed using trigonometry, thus eliminating the need for distance measurement, other than for setting out a baseline.

Survey by triangulation was used increasingly by surveyors following the introduction of the *plane-table* in 1551. This simple instrument consisted of a small drawing-board mounted on a tripod and equipped with a sighting rule or *alidade*. Using the alidade, the angles or directions between survey stations or points of detail could be plotted directly onto a sheet of paper pinned to the board. The technique became especially

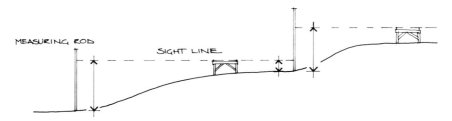

Figure 1.3 Using the chorobate to determine levels.

favoured by estate surveyors as no mathematical knowledge was required and plans could be produced with speed.

The *theodolite*, capable of measuring both horizontal and vertical angles, was first made in the early sixteenth century, its name being introduced by the English mathematician Leonard Digges (d. 1558). Later, telescope sights carrying cross-hairs and finely-graduated scales increased the standards of accuracy attainable. An improved understanding of geometry and trigonometry made triangulation and other calculations established surveying practice. By the late sixteenth century the science and practice of surveying had reached the stage where all the basic items of optical equipment available to the modern surveyor were in use.

As surveying theory developed into a practical occupation, treatises were produced, firstly for scientific explanation, and later as surveying manuals for the increasing numbers of apprentices in the seventeenth century. No new principles were introduced into surveying or cartography during the seventeenth or eighteenth centuries, although plane-tables, theodolites and levels were increasingly refined.

With the development of national transport systems, demand increased for surveyors capable of mapping land for acquisition and route-planning. The turnpike trusts and canal companies of the eighteenth century and the railway companies of the nineteenth century provided work for increasing numbers of surveyors, both for mapping and levelling.

Tacheometry was introduced as the basis for indirect distance measurement as early as the seventeenth century, where distances and heights were determined from instrument readings alone. The tacheometer, essentially a combined range-finding device and level, became popular with engineers engaged in rapid surveys for canals and railways in the early nineteenth century.

Today, the introduction of advanced technologies, notably those of computing and optoelectronics, has changed the practice of surveying both land and buildings, allowing high standards of dimensional accuracy to become readily available. When higher accuracies are required, it becomes necessary to combine linear and angular measurements to record the relationships of one point to another. This has traditionally been performed using a theodolite for measuring horizontal and vertical angles, and a tape or chain for horizontal distances. Electromagnetic distance measurement (EDM) systems have more recently been used to provide indirect linear measurements with accuracies of $\pm$ 5 mm, $\pm$ 5 p.p.m. Total station theodolites, that is theodolites with integrated EDM facilities, have become popular during the past decade.

The amount of data generated by a typical land survey has led to the introduction of portable computers and data-logging devices for storing readings in a form suitable for later restitution. This increased use of electronic and optical instrumentation in land surveying has recently been adopted for building recording, especially as the information is increasingly being used for other tasks such as analysis and interpretation. Increased demand for digital, rather than drawn, records has also promoted this form of surveying.

THE PRINCIPLES OF SURVEYING PRACTICE

Control

To produce a survey to a sufficient degree of accuracy for the purposes for which it is required, control points or survey stations are established. These points are fixed by measuring to a higher order of accuracy than is required for the finished product so that later lower-order work, to pick up detail, can be fitted and adjusted to a network of lines of sight (control lines), which run between the survey stations, without exceeding the tolerances set for the accuracy of the survey. The control framework, like a structural framework, should be adequately braced with extra survey stations if necessary, to ensure that it is sufficiently rigid and incapable of distortion. A tight network of control points is essential for high-order accuracy as all the detail will be based on it.

Economy of accuracy

The standard of accuracy worked to should be appropriate for the task and will be influenced by the scale of survey drawings that are to be prepared. The thickness of a fine pencil line is in the order of 0.2 mm and this sets an upper limit for the accuracy of any plot. If a building survey is to be plotted at a scale of 1 : 100, a dimension of 0.2 mm on paper will represent 0.2 × 100 = 20 mm on the building being measured. Thus detail need only be measured to the nearest 20 mm as a higher standard of measurement cannot be plotted and will be unnecessarily time-consuming, making the survey more expensive.

The following standards of measurement are suggested:

Table 1.1   Standards of measurement

Scale of survey drawing	Measure detail to the nearest mm
1 : 500	100
1 : 200	40
1 : 100	20
1 : 50	10
1 : 20	5

◆ *Consistency*. The various stages of a survey, control and detail fill-in must be properly co-ordinated as they will require different standards of accuracy. Each successive stage of a survey will be less accurate than the stage which preceded it. There is no advantage in measuring the fill-in detail to the same standard of accuracy as required for the initial framework, let alone a higher one.

◆ *Independent checks*. It is good survey practice to adopt procedures for fieldwork, calculations and plotting that are either self-checking or that provide an independent check.

◆ *Revision*. The method of working adopted for a survey should, if possible, readily facilitate revisions or extensions at a later date. Field-notes and computations should be clear, and kept together with photographs and other records for use by future surveyors, conservators or historians.

BASIC SURVEYING METHODS

Linear measurement

Linear measurement can be made in four ways, as described below.

Direct measurement

Using a measuring rod, tape or engineer's chain stretched between two points A and B.

Optical measurement

Distances may be measured optically by solving a triangle whose height is equal to the required distance.

Tacheometry   A surveyor's level or theodolite is set up on a tripod over point A and the telescope of the instrument sighted on a graduated staff at point B. The surveyor focuses on the staff and reads it against three cross-hairs seen through the eyepiece of the instrument (Figure 1.4). The distance between the top and bottom hairs, the *stadia distance*, is multiplied by a constant for the instrument, usually 100, to give the distance AB.

Subtense measurement   Two targets, usually two metres apart, are mounted at each end of a bar of invar steel (an alloy of iron and nickel having a very low coefficient of thermal expansion) which is fixed horizontally on a tripod over B (Figure 1.5). Using a theodolite positioned over A (Figure 1.6), the horizontal angle subtended by the targets is measured accurately (usually by averaging several readings) to reduce error:

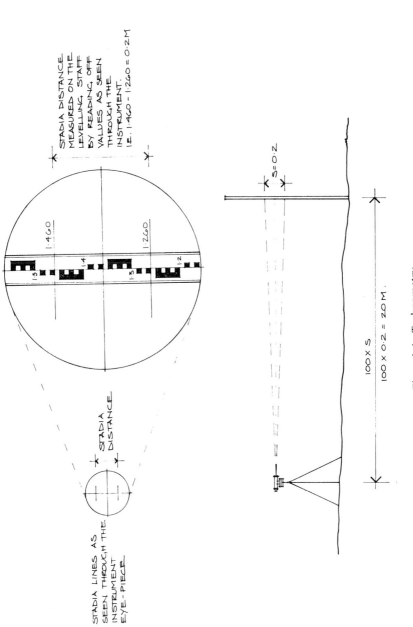

STADIA DISTANCE MEASURED ON THE LEVELLING STAFF BY READING OFF VALUES AS SEEN THROUGH THE INSTRUMENT. I.E. 1·460 - 1·260 = 0·2M

1·460

1·260

1·5

1·4

1·5

1·2

STADIA LINES AS SEEN THROUGH THE INSTRUMENT EYE-PIECE.

STADIA DISTANCE

S = 0·2

100 × S
100 × 0·2 = 20 M.

Figure 1.4 Tacheometry.

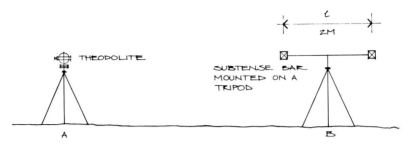

Figure 1.5 Subtense measurement.

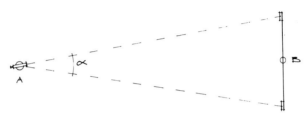

Figure 1.6 Measuring the horizontal angle subtended by the targets on the subtense bar.

AB = cot (α/2) × l/2
If l = 2 m
AB = cot (l/2) metres

The method is time-consuming and has been superseded by EDM.

Range finder The principle of this instrument is similar to that of subtense measurement, but with the fixed baseline built into the instrument. The surveyor, sighting through the range finder, sees two separate images from reflectors at the two ends of the fixed base within the instrument. By adjusting the base angles of the triangle the two images of the distant target are brought into coincidence, and the distance to the target read off. Range finders are not sufficiently accurate for most survey work.

Electromagnetic distance measurement (EDM)

A theodolite fitted with an EDM attachment or an independent EDM instrument is set up over A, and the theodolite or EDM sighted on a reflector positioned on B. EDM instruments work by calculating the phase difference between a transmitted signal of electromagnetic radiation and the reflected signal. This difference is the transit time which, when multiplied by the velocity of the signal, gives distance. The computation is performed by the instrument and distance displayed on a digital display.

Sonic measurement

The sonic tape works by emitting an ultra-sonic signal which is reflected from the surface it is aimed at. The pre-set frequency of the signal and the duration of the measured cycle allow the distance between the surfaces to be determined by the instrument and the result shown on a digital display. Distances up to 25 m may be measured single-handedly, but the accuracy is not sufficient for the preparation of detailed survey drawings.

The accuracy and reliability of sonic tapes is currently under discussion, though for single-handed linear measurement their usefulness is apparent.

Survey methods for supplying detail

Detail can be tied into a survey station or control framework by the following methods.

Offsetting

The position of the detail is fixed by taking a measurement to the detail, at right angles to a control line, and recording the position from which the offset is taken, relative to a survey station (Figure 1.7).

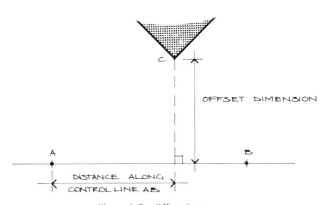

Figure 1.7   Offsetting.

Radiation (bearing and distance)

A theodolite is set up, usually at a survey station, and a bearing (the horizontal angle between the control line and the sightline to the detail) is observed. The distance from the survey station to the detail is recorded (Figure 1.8).

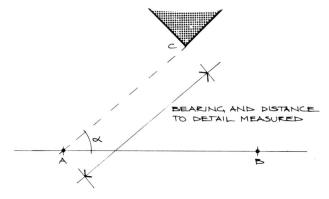

Figure 1.8   Radiation.

Triangulation

Using a control line as a base, bearings are taken on the detail from two different positions on the control line, usually the survey stations at each end (Figure 1.9). Using the length of the baseline, the lengths of the remaining two sides of the triangle formed by the instrument positions and the detail can be solved using the sine rule:

$$a/\sin A = b/\sin B = c/\sin C$$

If the baseline is c, then:

$$b = c \sin B \operatorname{cosec} C$$
$$a = c \sin A \operatorname{cosec} C$$

Alternatively, in a plane-table survey the angles and the position of the detail can be established graphically.

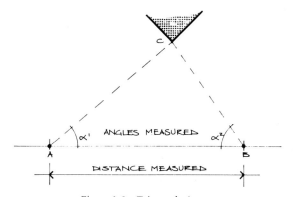

Figure 1.9   Triangulation.

Trilateration

Using the control line as a base, measurements are taken to the detail from two different known positions on that baseline (Figure 1.10). The triangle so formed, of which all the side lengths are known, can either be solved by trigonometry or graphically. The latter method is commonly used for chain and building surveys.

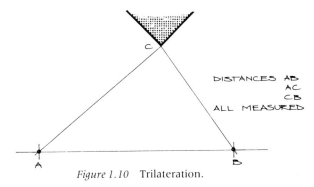

Figure 1.10 Trilateration.

Height measurement

Levelling

The most common method of determining the gradients of a site, and the relative levels of floors in a building, is to use a surveyor's level and staff. In essence, the level is a tripod-mounted telescope which can be adjusted so that the line of sight in any direction through the telescope is truly horizontal. The base of the staff, a three or four metre measuring rod, graduated at ten millimetre intervals, is held vertically on those surfaces whose height is required. By observing the staff through the cross-hairs in the telescope the heights of features can be measured relative to the line of sight. When the level has to be moved to a new position to take further observations, the staff remains held at the feature where the last reading was taken. Once the instrument has been set up in a new position, a second reading is taken on the staff before it is moved on for further observations. The levels of the various features relative to a known datum may be calculated from the readings taken (Figure 1.11).

Trigonometric heighting

This method uses a theodolite to measure vertical angles relative to a horizontal plane. If the slope or horizontal distance to a detail is known then the difference in height can be calculated by trigonometry. The method is not as accurate as levelling, but can be useful on steeply sloping

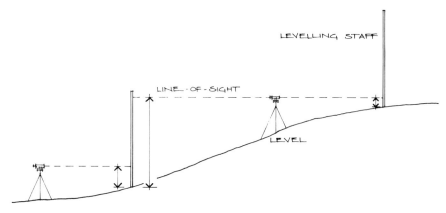

Figure 1.11 Levelling.

sites or for measuring the heights of features such as church steeples (Figure 1.12).

Water level

The water level method relies on the fact that water finds its own level. Water levels are composed of a length of rubber hose with a clear plastic or glass tube at each end. The apparatus is filled with water, taking care to remove any air bubbles. A datum is selected and the water level at one end of the apparatus lined up with it. The other end of the apparatus can now be used to transfer this datum level to other locations, which do not need to be in visual contact with the first (Figure 1.13). Features such as floor and ceiling levels above and below the established datum can now be measured in. The method has the virtue of being simple and the equipment cheap; but it is laborious to use and prone to error (airlocks, the hose becoming pinched or leaks).

SOURCES OF INACCURACY IN SURVEY WORK

All survey work is liable to error, whether it be in the taking of measurements (linear or angular), computation or plotting. To reduce the possibility of error and inaccuracy to a minimum, sound survey practices and methods of working, as described in the following chapters, should be followed. Some common sources of error are described below.

Carelessness

Carelessness on the part of the surveyor such as misreading an observation,

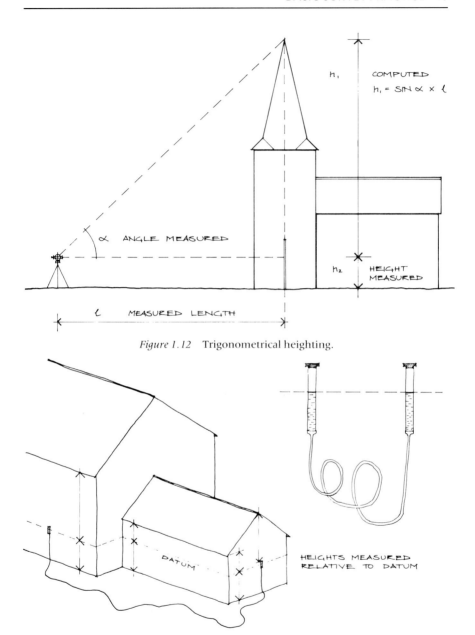

h_1 COMPUTED

$h_1 = \text{SIN} \propto \times \ell$

$\propto$ ANGLE MEASURED

h_2 HEIGHT MEASURED

ℓ MEASURED LENGTH

Figure 1.12   Trigonometrical heighting.

DATUM

HEIGHTS MEASURED RELATIVE TO DATUM

Figure 1.13   Water level.

failing to set up an instrument correctly, transposing figures during booking or computation.

Constant errors

Constant errors occur due to the limitations of the equipment being used.

A linentape, for example, may become stretched by use and thus be too long. This means that for every full tape length measured there will be a consistent negative error as it will measure the line shorter than it actually is. When measuring a long line, the error will be cumulative. Constant errors can be prevented by standardizing the equipment and making suitable corrections.

Systematic errors

Systematic errors, like constant errors, always occur under the same set of conditions and may be either positive or negative, but are variable rather than constant. For example, in taping a long line between two survey stations the tape may become slightly misaligned in each tape length. The misalignment will give rise to negative errors which will vary from tape length to tape length. The error will be cumulative. Systematic errors can be guarded against by adopting sound methods of working.

Periodic errors

Periodic errors are errors which may be eliminated by good operational practice. For example, the line of sight through the telescope of a theodolite may not be truly at right angles to the trunnion axis of the instrument. However, if both face left and face right readings are taken, the mean angle from pairs of observations will eliminate any error (Figure 1.14).

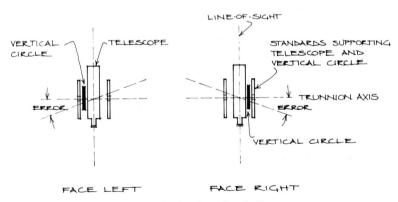

Figure 1.14 Elimination of periodic errors.

CHAPTER TWO

Surveying Equipment

This chapter describes the surveying equipment commonly employed in measured survey work, together with notes on its use. Subsequent chapters deal in greater detail with the techniques of using the equipment. Many of the instruments described are illustrated in Figure 2.1.

Abney level

A type of *clinometer* which is used to measure vertical angles. This hand-held instrument consists of a rectangular sighting tube incorporating a mirror, so that a bubble tube, attached to it, can be observed in coincidence with the object being sighted (Figure 2.2). The object is observed, and the bubble tube, which is pivoted, is adjusted so that the bubble is bisected by the instrument's cross-hair. The vertical angle is indicated by a pointer arm which moves across a graduated arc as the bubble tube is moved. Using the vernier scale and magnifying glass provided, readings may be estimated to ten minutes of arc. Its main use is for low-order accuracy work, such as measuring the slope angle on chain surveys or calculating the height of tall features such as factory chimneys.

Chain

The surveyor's chain was invented by the English mathematician Edmund Gunter (1581–1626) to provide a robust method of making linear measurements over rough ground. It consists of heavy wire links joined together by oval rings and has swivelling brass 'D' handles at each end.

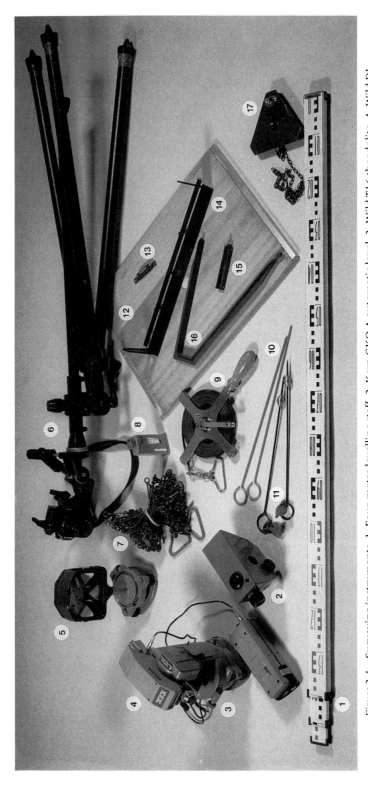

Figure 2.1 Surveying instruments. 1. Four-metre levelling staff. 2. Kern GKO A automatic level. 3. Wild T16 theodolite. 4. Wild DI 1000 EDM unit. 5. Wild EDM prism. 6. Thirty-five millimetre camera and tripod. 7. Twenty-metre land chain. 8. Constant tension handle. 9. Thirty-metre steel band. 10. Chaining arrows. 11. Drop arrows. 12. Plane-table. 13. Board level. 14. Alidade. 15. Trough compass. 16. Plumbing fork. 17. Change plate.

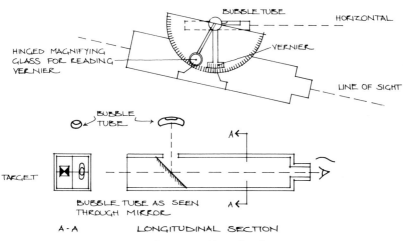

Figure 2.2 Abney level.

Modern metric chains consist of one hundred links and measure twenty metres overall when stretched out. The chain is marked every metre with a yellow tally except at the five, ten and fifteen metre positions, where a red tally is used.

A chaining party consisting of a surveyor and an assistant work as follows:

1. The surveyor, holding one end of the chain (or tape) at a survey station, sends the assistant forward to the other end of the chain with ten *chaining arrows*, to be lined in with the distant survey station.
2. With the chain lined in, and fully stretched out, the assistant marks the position of the end of the chain by pushing an arrow into the ground. On hard paving a chalk mark is made and an arrow placed adjacent.
3. Detail is picked up by the surveyor moving along the chain line and offsetting from it with a tape.
4. When the surveyor reaches the end of the chain the assistant is sent forward, dragging the chain behind, to measure out the next length. Before moving forward the surveyor picks up the arrow and thus has a reminder of the number of chain lengths that have been completed. The procedure is repeated until the line length has been surveyed.

Chaining arrow

A chaining arrow is a steel pin used when chaining to mark the end of a tape or chain. So that arrows can be easily seen, a strip of red cloth is tied to them at the top.

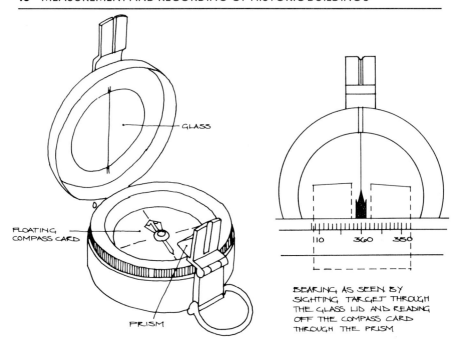

GLASS

FLOATING
COMPASS CARD

PRISM

110   360   350

BEARING AS SEEN BY
SIGHTING TARGET THROUGH
THE GLASS LID AND READING
OFF THE COMPASS CARD
THROUGH THE PRISM

Figure 2.3   Prismatic compass.

Change plate

A triangular steel plate used for supporting the base of a *levelling staff* on soft ground especially at *change points*.

Clinometer

A simple instrument for measuring vertical angles.

Compass

For many centuries the earth's magnetic field and the compass provided surveyors and navigators with their only means of measuring angles and directions. They are still useful today for orientating a survey and for conducting preliminary surveys and rough mapping.

A small, hand-held prismatic compass, of the type most useful for survey work, consists of a card which floats in a heavy liquid and is graduated around its edge into the 360 degrees of the circle (Figure 2.3). A bearing is taken by opening the lid of the compass, roughly at right angles to its body, and sighting through a prism (which is attached to the body by a hinge). The surveyor, looking through the prism, moves the compass until the survey target is bisected by the hairline fixed to the lid and simultaneously observes the bearing on the card below. Bearings can be read to the nearest thirty minutes and perhaps estimated to the nearest fifteen minutes.

Corner offset

Electromagnetic distance measurement involves the reflection of an infra-red beam from the instrument via a prism mounted on the detail pole. When recording building corners and other vertical features, it is not normally possible to place the prism directly over the feature. A corner offset, fabricated from plastic or hardboard, is used to move the prism a fixed distance (say 100 mm) from both external and internal corners. The face of the building can be plotted by taking into account the offset at the draughting stage.

Data logger

Any electronic device for recording and transferring measured survey data. Hand-held examples may be used as electronic field-books with the surveyor typing in measurements, although they are more commonly used to accept data directly from electronic survey equipment.

Detail pole

Telescopic rod (usually two metres long) used for mounting an EDM prism.

Diagonal eyepiece

Theodolite eyepiece attachment used for taking sightings closer to vertical than is possible with a standard eyepiece.

Digital terrain model (DTM)

A computer-generated surface model used as a basis for automatic contour interpolation and site visualization (Figure 2.4).

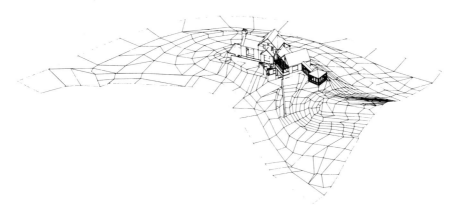

Figure 2.4   Digital terrain model.

Drop arrow

When chaining on sloping sites it is usual to chain downhill, pulling the chain taut and holding it horizontal. At intervals not exceeding twenty metres, the dimension is plumbed down to the ground level using a weighted or drop arrow. Thus the chaining continues in a series of steps down the slope.

Electromagnetic distance measurement (EDM)

EDM is an indirect method of measurement incorporating the reflection of a beam of infra-red light from the prism which is placed over the target. Typical equipment has a range of over one kilometre with a standard error of less than ten millimetres.

Global positioning systems (GPS)

GPS represents a rapidly evolving technology which provides the 3D coordinates of a GPS receiver by calculating from data received from satellites. Such systems can determine positions of points on the earth's surface to within one metre. Although currently suffering from disjointed satellite coverage, future developments will rectify many of the problems and provide a possibility for use in site surveys.

Level

A level consists of a telescope with a spirit level attached to it in such a manner that, when its bubble is centred, the line of sight is horizontal. The telescope has a vertical cross-hair for sighting on points and a horizontal one with which readings are made from a *levelling staff*. In addition, stadia hairs may also be present for tacheometry.

The three basic types of level are: dumpy, tilting and automatic.

Dumpy level The spirit level is attached to the telescope, which should also be perpendicular to the vertical axis of the instrument, and parallel to the line of sight (or line of collimation). The telescope is brought to the horizontal plane by using three levelling screws on the *tribrach*, or *levelling head* (Figure 2.5).

The procedure for setting up a dumpy level ready for use is as follows:

1. Set up the *tripod* with the legs about one metre apart, adjusting their length as necessary so that the top is approximately level, and at a comfortable height for the surveyor to read the instrument that will be mounted on it.

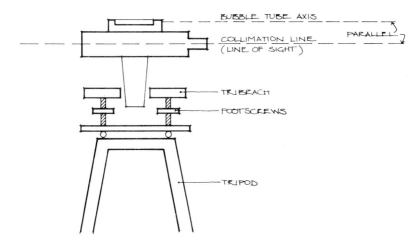

Figure 2.5   Dumpy level.

2. Ensure that the tripod is firm by treading the legs into soft ground or using a *star* on hard paving.
3. Level the instrument using the three footscrews as follows:
    (a) Lay the telescope parallel to two footscrews and centre the spirit level bubble by slowly turning footscrews at the same speed in opposite directions. The bubble will move in the same direction as the surveyor's left thumb.
    (b) Turn the telescope through 90 degrees and centre the bubble using the third footscrew only.
    (c) Repeat (a) and (b) until the bubble remains centred.
    (d) Turn the telescope through 180 degrees, if the bubble stays centred the instrument is levelled up and ready to use.

Tilting level   The tilting level is one in which the telescope can be rotated about its horizontal axis (Figure 2.6). The tilting level is set up

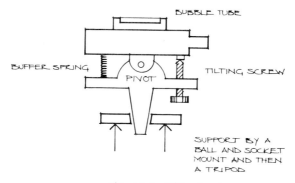

Figure 2.6   Tilting level.

approximately using a circular or bull's eye spirit level. This initial setting up operation is effected either by using three footscrews (as described for the dumpy level) or, more usually, by a *ball and socket mount* which is commonly used by instrument makers instead of a *tribrach*. The final levelling up is carried out by tilting the telescope using the *gradienter screw* until the telescope bubble, as viewed either by a mirror or split bubble prism, is centred. Where a split bubble prism is used, the bubble is observed through a separate eyepiece in which both ends of the bubble can be seen, the instrument being level when the two halves of the bubble coincide. The tilting level can be set up faster than a dumpy, but the surveyor must be sure to centre the telescope bubble on a distant levelling staff before every observation.

Automatic levels The automatic level is fitted with a ball and socket mount and roughly levelled using a circular spirit level. By means of a *compensator*, a prismatic device suspended on fine wires, the instrument itself will carry out the final levelling up.

Levelling staff

Levelling staffs are used to measure the vertical distance between a point of detail on which they are held, and the line of sight (collimation) of a level instrument. The face of a metric staff is graduated at intervals of ten millimetres, the base of the staff being zero, and may be read by estimation to the nearest one millimetre. Imperial staffs are graduated at intervals of

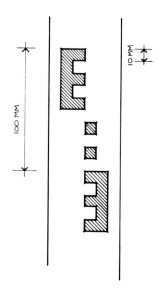

Figure 2.7   E pattern staff graduations.

one-tenth of a foot. The most commonly used staff graduation pattern in the UK is the BS 4484 'E' pattern (Figure 2.7).

A circular spirit level or *staff bubble* may be fitted to the staff to ensure that the staff is vertical when readings are being taken.

For ease of transportation, such as in a car boot, the staffs may be telescopic, hinged or made up of sections that join together.

Optical square

The optical square is an instrument which allows the surveyor simultaneously to observe along a line of sight and at right angles to it. The most convenient type consists of two pentagonal prisms mounted one above the other (Figure 2.8).

The optical square may be used for setting up right angles or taking offsets. When setting up a right angle, the surveyor stands at the required point on, say, a chain line and sights the ranging rod marking the survey station at its end. By observing through the prism of the optical square, the surveyor can direct the assistant holding a ranging rod to move backwards and forwards parallel to the chain line until the ranging rod, seen through

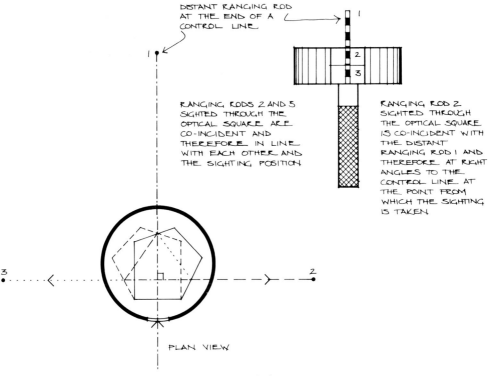

Figure 2.8 Optical square.

the prism, lines up with the rod at the survey station. When the rods are in line, the assistant marks the point by pushing the rod vertically into the ground. Offsets are taken with the assistant holding a ranging rod on the detail to be measured in, and the surveyor moving along the chain line until the assistant's rod, as viewed through the optical square, appears to be in alignment with the rod at the survey station.

The double prism optical square can also be used as a *line ranger*, which enables the surveyor to establish an intermediate point, in line with and in between two distant survey stations, without the necessity of sighting from one of them. To locate the intermediate point, the surveyor walks backwards and forwards across the line, and at right angles to it, with the instrument up to the eye. The intermediate point is established when the *image of each ranging rod* marking one end of the line appears in its respective prism to be vertically in line with the other.

Plane-table

The plane-table consists of a small drawing board, mounted on a tripod, equipped with a sighting rule or *alidade*. Using the alidade, the angles or directions between survey stations, or points of detail, can be plotted directly onto a sheet of paper pinned to the board, and scaled using a rule which forms part of the alidade. The simplest type of plane table has an alidade provided with basic sighting vanes, more sophisticated alidades have a telescope with stadia hairs for tacheometry. The plane-table is set up over the survey station using a *plumb-bob* suspended from a *plumbing fork*, and the table levelled using a spirit level. The main advantage of the plane-table is that the surveyor can compare the plot with the actual features on the ground as work proceeds.

Plumb-bob

A weighted string (the plumb-line) used to show a vertical line.

Ranging rods

Ranging rods are poles, two metres high and pointed at one end for pushing into the ground. They are used for marking the positions of survey stations and intermediate points along a survey line. On hard, paved surfaces a tripod support is used to hold the rod in a vertical position. They are usually painted red and white, in bands 200 mm deep, to make them easily visible. Ranging rods are available made in timber, metal and plastic, and for ease of transportation may be made in two pieces which join together.

Star

A star is a device with three arms, each connected at one end to a central node. It is used to prevent the legs of a tripod slipping on hard, paved surfaces. The star is placed on the ground and each foot of the tripod placed in a loop at the end of the arms.

Steel band

Steel bands are most commonly thirty, fifty or one hundred metres long and carried on a cruciform winding reel. Steel bands are much lighter than chains and are used where a high order of accuracy is required. For accurate work a standard tension is applied using a spring balance or *tension handle*, and corrections are made for temperature. Very accurate work is executed using *catenary* rather than surface taping. In catenary taping the tape is suspended and a correction made for the sag.

Steel bands are quite strong but must be kept straight because they are easily broken if they become looped or kinked. After use in wet conditions, the band must be dried with a cloth and then wiped with an oily rag to prevent rusting.

Steel tape

The steel tape is similar to the steel band but is wound into a case rather than onto a reel. The most commonly used length for chain survey work is twenty metres. A small three or five metre pocket tape is useful for measuring building detail.

Surveyor's rod (or rule)

A two metre, folding, boxwood rule. Rods are generally either twofold or sixfold.

Tacheometer

A theodolite modified to facilitate indirect distance measurement. Horizontal distances and height differences from the instrument are derived from readings taken onto a staff placed over the target point.

Tension handle

When using tapes and bands to measure distances it may be appropriate, depending upon the accuracy required, to take into account the tension being applied. A tension handle incorporates a tape grip and a spring balance to provide such data.

Telescopic rod

An alternative to the traditional surveyor's folding rod. Telescopic rods are available which can measure up to five metres and are particularly useful for measuring floor to ceiling heights or for single-handed measurement of small rooms.

Theodolite

The theodolite is a precision instrument for measuring both horizontal and vertical angles (Figure 2.9). It is used with a tripod and levelled up using footscrews as described for the dumpy level.

A theodolite is constructed as follows. A *lower plate* supports a graduated horizontal circle. An *upper plate* rotates with respect to the lower plate and has an index pointer which may be laid against any graduation on the lower plate. A general-purpose theodolite can be read directly to twenty seconds of arc; a typical builder's theodolite for low-order work can be read to one minute of arc and be estimated to thirty seconds. The upper plate supports two *A frames*, or *standards*, which contain the optical systems for

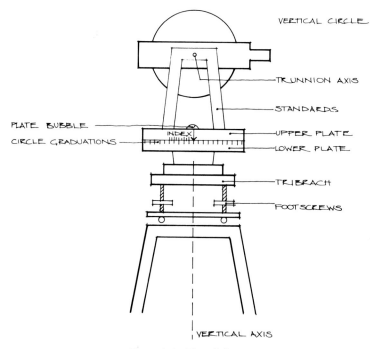

Figure 2.9 Theodolite.

reading the circles in addition to supporting the telescope of the instrument and the vertical circle. On top of the upper plate is the *horizontal plate bubble* which is used for levelling the instrument when setting up.

The telescope and the vertical circle are carried by, and rotate in a vertical plane about, the *trunnion axis*. The telescope is said to be 'transitted' when it is turned vertical through 180 degrees. By transitting the telescope and then 'swinging' it horizontally through 180 degrees the vertical circle initially on the left-hand side of the telescope appears on the right-hand side after the reversal. By observing a horizontal angle with the instrument in the face left position, and then changing face, by transitting and swinging the telescope, to make a further observation with the instrument face right, a more accurate measurement of the angle is possible. The mean angle obtained from the two observations will minimize instrument errors, such as dislevelment of the trunnion axis, circle eccentricity and the collimation axis not being at right angles to the trunnion axis. In addition, the procedure provides a check on the surveyor's readings.

Vertical angles are measured by a graduated circle attached to the telescope and perpendicular to the trunnion axis. The *vertical circle* reads zero when the line of sight of the telescope is horizontal, and the vertical angle (elevation or depression) is measured relative to the horizontal.

The theodolite must be accurately centred over the survey station. Traditionally this is done with the *plumb-bob*, with which all instruments are supplied. Modern instruments are usually provided with an *optical plummet* too, comprising a small telescope which, by means of a prism, enables the surveyor to view the ground-mark. The optical plummet has obvious advantages over the plumb-bob in windy conditions.

Centring rods are available for some modern theodolites and are in the form of an extendable rod attached to the instrument mount in place of a plumb-bob. The end of the rod is placed on the survey station and is brought to a vertical position either by adjusting the tripod legs or by unclamping the tribrach and sliding it across the tripod head. The verticality of the centring rod is checked by a circular level bubble fitted to the rod. Centring rods are graduated so that the height of the instrument above the survey station can be read directly from it.

The various movements of the theodolite are controlled by *clamps* and associated slow-motion *screws*.

Total station

The total station is an instrument which integrates the features of an electronic theodolite with an electromagnetic distance measurement facility.

Tribrach

The tribrach is a levelling head which is found at the base of theodolites and many levels. It is used with its associated footscrews for levelling up the instrument ready for use.

Tripod

Tripods are three-legged stands for supporting instruments such as levels, plane-tables and theodolites. A good tripod should combine lightness and portability with rigidity when in use. Most tripods have timber or metal legs which are adjustable in length and hinged at their tops to a metal tripod head. Tripod heads vary in design: some have a captive bolt which is screwed into the tribrach of the instrument, whilst others incorporate the tribrach itself.

Woven tapes

Woven tapes are made of strong synthetic fibres which are covered with a water-resistant plastic coating. They are prone to stretching and shrinkage in use and are not suitable for very precise measurement. Their main use is for measuring inside buildings where a steel tape is more prone to being broken in confined spaces.

CHAPTER THREE

Elementary Land Survey

A building cannot be divorced from its site, and most commissions to survey a building will require the immediate surroundings to be recorded also. Elementary land survey techniques using simple equipment and suitable for recording small sites are described below.

CHAIN SURVEY

Measurement by chain survey is suitable for small areas of land. It uses direct linear measurement alone and no angles are measured.

A *control framework* of triangles, formed by *chain lines* linking up *control points* or *survey stations*, is established on the site and the distances between the control points measured by chain, tape or band. *Detail* can be picked up from this framework by taking *offsets* or *ties* at measured distances along the chain line.

Principles of setting up the control framework

1. Select a *baseline* upon which to build up the control framework. The baseline should be as long as possible and all triangles should be based on it, or tied back to it.
2. The triangles in the framework should be well conditioned, i.e. no angle should be greater than 120 degrees or less than 30 degrees.
3. The chain lines should run as close to the detail as is practicable in order to reduce the length of offsets. The lines should also run across ground which is clear of obstacles and as level as possible. Additional lines not

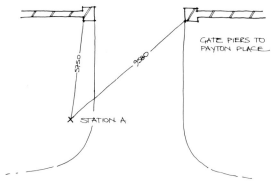

Figure 3.1 Safeguarding.

forming part of the control framework are added specifically to pick up detail: these are known as *detail lines*.

4. To 'prove' each triangle, an extra line or *check line* should be introduced and measured.
5. The number of lines should be kept to a minimum consistent with accuracy.
6. Control points should be marked on the ground. In soft ground a timber peg is used and on paved surfaces a nail may be driven between paving slabs. It is good survey practice to *safeguard* the control point by taking measurements from it to adjacent permanent features so that it can be easily found at some future date or relocated if moved or destroyed during the survey itself (Figure 3.1).

Equipment

The basic equipment for a chain survey is:

> Chain (or steel band for high-order work)
> Chaining arrows
> Optical square
> Ranging rods
> Woven tape
> Lump hammer, pegs, nails, chalk

Additional equipment may be taken according to the specific requirements of the survey.

Reconnaissance

It is advisable to visit the site prior to the survey proper in order to assess the task and:

1. To estimate the time (and cost) of the survey.

2. To plan out a strategy for conducting the survey. A large survey often takes several days and involves more than one survey team. The extent of each day's work and the responsibilities of each team should be co-ordinated and planned.

3. To identify any potential difficulties or hazards and make suitable arrangements. For example, to obtain permission to enter land of third parties; or, if working near busy main roads, to have available warning signs and fluorescent coats or vests.

4. To decide on any special equipment that may be needed.

During the reconnaissance it is useful to have a photocopied extract from a large-scale Ordnance Survey (OS) sheet (1 : 1250) showing the site. Extracts which have been enlarged on a photocopier are particularly useful for planning out a control framework and for making notes on.

Survey procedure

1. First of all the control framework is established, ensuring that only well-conditioned triangles are used, and each control point marked with a peg. The control framework should be recorded either on a rough sketch or on an OS extract which will act as an index to the fieldwork notes. Each control point should be given a reference letter. Figure 3.2 shows a typical sketch of a control framework. The figures above each control line record the measured length of the line, using the convention that the starting point for the measurement is to the left of the figured dimension, when the sketch is viewed with the dimensions the right way up for normal reading. The figures below the control lines refer to the page numbers on the booking sheets where the full dimensional details will be found.

2. Starting at a suitable control point, a control line is selected for measurement, and the control point at each end is marked with a ranging rod. With the surveyor standing on one end of the chain at a control point, the assistant moves towards the distant control point with the other end of the chain. When the chain is fully stretched, the surveyor sights the ranging rod at the far end of the line and directs the assistant by hand signals to move to the left or right until lined in. A ranging rod may be held vertically by the assistant to help the surveyor with the lining in. The chain is then stretched taut with the surveyor's end placed precisely at the control point and the assistant marking the other end with a chaining arrow.

3. Next, starting at the control point, the surveyor and the assistant measure in detail to either side of the chain line. Using a steel band or tape, with the surveyor holding the ring end and the assistant the tape box, offsets are raised to the detail. The surveyor checks that each offset is perpendicular, usually by eye, and notes the chainage and the offset

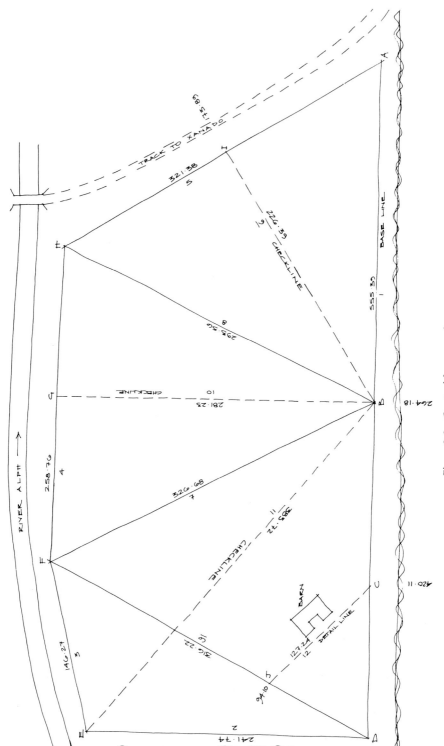

Figure 3.2 Control framework.

Table 3.1 Maximum recommended offset lengths

Plotting scale	Max. length of offset (m) to:	
	distinct points of detail e.g. corners of buildings	indefinite detail e.g. meandering streams
1:500 1:1000 1:1250	8	16
1:2000 1:2500	16	20

distance called out by the assistant. Where a long offset has to be raised it is advisable to do so using an optical square.

If two or more points of detail lie along the offset, for example the two sides of a footpath, *running offsets* are taken. That is to say, the successive measurements to each point of detail are measured from the same starting point, i.e. the chain line. *Running dimensions* are commonly used in survey work in preference to a string of separate dimensions which measure individual distances between successive points of detail, as running dimensions are more convenient to take, avoid cumulative error and are easier to use when plotting. The length of offsets to detail should be limited (see Table 3.1) to ensure that the survey measurements are compatible with the accuracy demanded in the plotting.

Where the detail is some distance from the chain line, more accurate results may be obtained by using *braced offsets* (also known as *ties* or *tie lines*). In this method, measurements to a common point of detail are taken from two or more positions along the chain line: unlike perpendicular offsets, braced offsets can be taken at any angle to the chain line.

If features have straight lines, such as the sides of buildings, and are close to the chain line, it is usual for the surveyor to note the chainage at which the alignment of the feature, if produced, would cut the chain line. Such *straights* may be measured or unmeasured.

When the position of the wall of a rectangular building has been picked up by offsets (and possibly straights), the other sides of the building can be supplied by *plus measurements*.

4. When the end of the chain line is reached, the assistant drags the chain forward and the procedure is repeated until the whole length of the control line has been measured.

Booking procedure

Dimensions should be recorded either in a *chain survey book*, or on A4 *booking sheets*. In both cases the paper is ruled down the centre of each sheet with two parallel lines approximately fifteen millimetres apart which represent the chain line.

Clarity and accuracy are essential, so it is necessary to cultivate neat and methodical booking habits.

1. Start with details of the location of the survey, the job reference, date, surveyor's name, and so forth.
2. Sketch the control framework, identifying control points, etc.
3. Start a fresh page/sheet for each control, check or detail line.
4. Enter the chainage dimensions between the parallel lines.
5. Starting at the bottom of the page, neatly sketch the detail (approximately to scale) on either side of the central column according to which side of the chain line it is on. It is usual to start at the bottom of the sheet and work up the page so that the detail is always being recorded in the same direction as the chaining measurements.
6. All measurements are usually taken in metres, generally to one decimal place, or two if buildings are concerned.

Booking conventions are illustrated in Figure 3.3.

PLOTTING PROCEDURES

The following equipment is required for plotting a chain survey and producing the finished drawing:

> Drawing-board
> Tee square and/or a steel straightedge
> Set square
> Scale rule
> Beam compasses
> Pencils and technical pens
> Eraser
> Stencils
> Dry transfer material (lettering, tones)
> Paper
> Draughting tape

Plotting the survey

1. Prepare the drawing-board with a sheet of cartridge or layout paper held in place with draughting tape. With the aid of a tee square, draw a pencil line along the bottom of the drawing sheet and, using an appropriate scale, mark off and note the lengths of the various chain lines to be plotted (Figure 3.4).

COMMENTARY

EXTRACT FROM BOOKING SHEET

LENGTH OF CHAIN EMPHASIZED BY ENTERING SIDEWAYS BETWEEN THE PARALLEL LINES AND 'TOPPING & TAILING'

THE CURVING FENCE LINE IS MEASURED BY TAKING OFFSETS AT REGULAR INTERVALS

PLUS MEASUREMENTS MADE AT RIGHT ANGLES TO A LENGTH OF STRAIGHT DETAIL - USEFUL FOR SUPPLYING DETAIL OF RECTANGULAR BUILDINGS. PLUS SIGN ENTERED NEAREST THE POINT OF DETAIL AT WHICH THE PLUS DIMENSION IS TAKEN

NOTE HOW DETAIL IS SHOWN WHERE A PATH CROSSES THE CHAIN LINE OBLIQUELY

UNMEASURED STRAIGHT SHOWN AS A PECKED LINE - CHAINAGE AT THE POINT OF INTERCEPT CIRCLED

MEASURED STRAIGHTS SHOWN AS PECKED LINES WITH THE MEASURED LENGTH PLACED IN A CIRCLE

BRACED OFFSETS TO A TREE INDICATED BY PECKED LINE

RUNNING OFFSETS AT CHAINAGE 4.20 M

OFFSET OF 3.50 M AT CHAINAGE 0.00 M

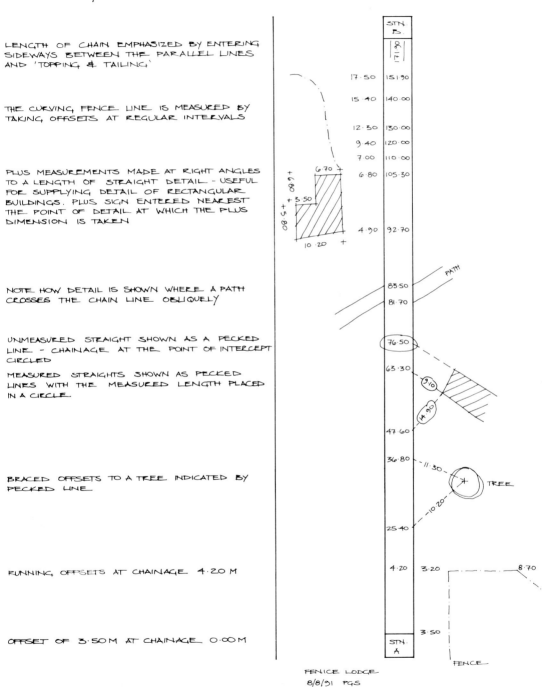

FENICE LODGE
8/8/91 PGS

Figure 3.3 Booking a chainline.

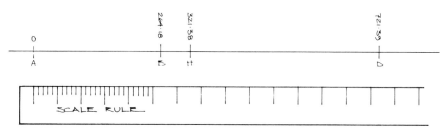

Figure 3.4   Scale line.

2. The first chain line to be plotted is the *baseline*. It should be drawn in pencil, using the tee square or straightedge, at a suitable position on the drawing sheet. The baseline is scaled to length using beam compasses, which have had their points adjusted to the correct distance apart by reference to the scale line plotted along the bottom of the drawing sheet (Figure 3.5). The appropriate length is marked off on the baseline by swinging arcs with the beam compasses, thus accurately defining each end of the line.

3. The largest and best conditioned triangle tied to the baseline is plotted next, using the beam compasses to swing scaled arcs from each end of the baseline, to define the point where the other two sides of the triangle intersect. When drawing in these sides, with the edge of a tee square or a straightedge, care must be taken to ensure the lines drawn pass accurately through the plotted point.

4. Further triangles are plotted, as described above, until the whole

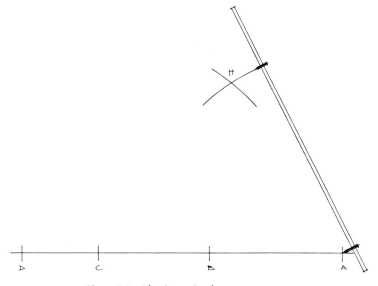

Figure 3.5   Plotting using beam compasses.

control framework of chain lines has been completed. Measuring the check lines, and comparing the values obtained with those in the field-notes, provides a check on the accuracy. Measured line lengths are generally acceptable within a tolerance limit of 1 : 500.

At this point any errors will be apparent and must be rectified before proceeding to plot in the detail. If the misclosure of plotted lines is large, remeasurement will be necessary. Small misclosures may be dealt with by the judicious adjustment of the lines affected, i.e. by slightly lengthening or shortening them as appropriate.

5. Detail is added by scaling and marking on the plotted control lines the positions at which offsets were raised. The offsets themselves are drawn at right angles to the control line by using a straightedge and a small set square. The appropriate dimensions are scaled off to plot the position of the detail (Figure 3.6).

Common errors to be guarded against in plotting detail are:

1. Plotting from the wrong end of the control line.
2. Plotting the offset on the wrong side of the control line.
3. Plotting the offset from the wrong point.
4. Omitting offsets altogether.

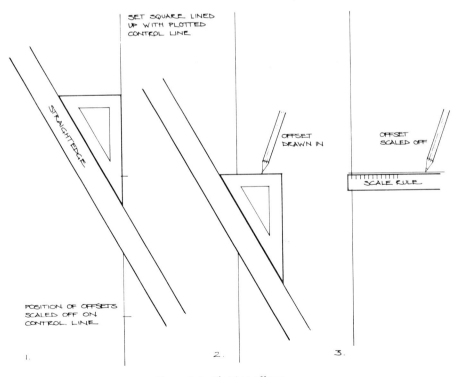

Figure 3.6 Plotting offsets.

PREPARING THE FINISHED SURVEY DRAWING

When the plot is complete, it can be traced onto tracing paper or polyester film to form the final drawing, which can then be used as a negative to produce further copies by *dyeline* process, or by *photocopying*.

1. A suitable sized drawing sheet of tracing paper or film is placed over the plotting sheet and secured in place with draughting tape. Care should be taken to position the survey plan so that the finished sheet will be well composed and balanced, with sufficient space left around the drawing for titling and annotation. By convention, land surveys are drawn with grid north at the top of the sheet.

2. In tracing the plot, in ink or pencil, it is usual to show the detail only, and to omit the positions of control points and lines. Some of the symbols conventionally adopted to indicate various features on plans are shown in Figure 3.7. The survey drawing may also be enhanced by the use of block shading or hatching (either drawn by hand or using rub-down dry transfer such as Letratone™) to define differing areas of vegetation, paved areas, and so on.

3. The survey drawing is annotated to give the names and descriptions of the various features shown. Such annotation can be applied by means of freehand lettering, stencils or rub-down dry transfer lettering such as Letraset™.

4. In order that the plan may be correctly orientated, a north point must be added in a convenient position on the drawing.

5. Finally, a border and a title panel are added. The title panel should contain the following information:

1. Title, indicating the sheet content, for example *Survey of Mansfield Park, Northamptonshire*.
2. The scale as a representative fraction, 1:500, say, and possibly a metric and/or an imperial scale bar.
3. The date of the survey and plotting if separated by a length of time.
4. Name(s) of the surveyor(s), and who has checked the drawing.
5. Job/drawing reference number.
6. Any other relevant information, for example the measurement technique used so that future surveyors can assess relative degrees of accuracy.

Readers not familiar with architectural draughting and drawing conventions should refer to BS 1192 *Construction Drawing Practice*, British Standards Institution (1984), and the relevant texts listed in the bibliography.

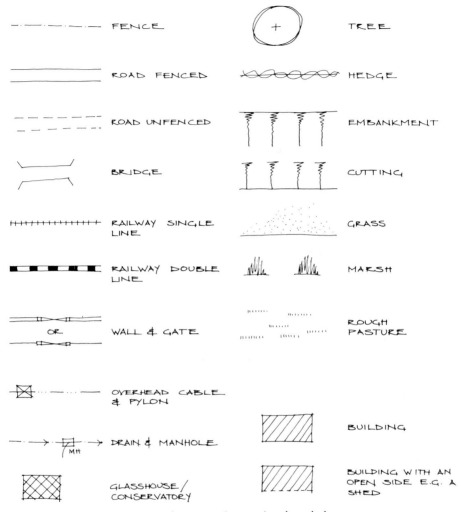

Figure 3.7 Conventional symbols.

PLANE-TABLE SURVEYING

The plane-table is a simple instrument which allows the angles or directions between survey control points to be simultaneously observed and plotted in the field. The basic equipment is illustrated in Figure 3.8.

In essence, the plane-table is a tripod-mounted drawing-board approximately 600 × 600 mm in size which can be levelled and rotated about a vertical axis and clamped into any position. It is used in conjunction with an *alidade* which is sighted onto survey stations and points of detail.

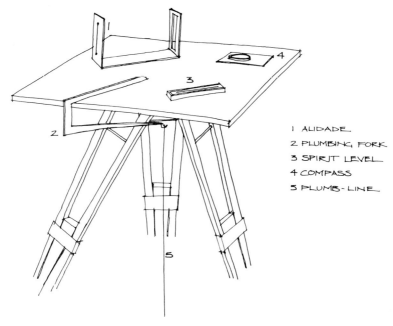

1 ALIDADE
2 PLUMBING FORK
3 SPIRIT LEVEL
4 COMPASS
5 PLUMB-LINE

Figure 3.8 Plane-table.

Procedures for using the plane-table

1. The tripod is set up over a survey station (marked by a timber peg in soft ground or a nail in paved surfaces) and the table adjusted, with the aid of a spirit level, until perfectly horizontal.

2. Good quality drawing paper is firmly fixed to the plane-table with draughting tape. A pencil mark is made on the paper to represent the instrument station. If the survey is to be done at a large scale, where the size of the board is significant in relation to the lengths of the sights, the upper point of a plumbing fork is placed at the point marking the instrument station and the table adjusted so that the plumb-bob attached to the lower part of the fork is directly over the ground mark.

3. There are three methods of surveying using a plane-table: *radiation*, *intersection* and *traversing*.

♦ *Radiation*. The plane-table is set up at a central station and, with the ruling edge of the alidade placed against the mark representing the instrument station, the points of detail sighted on. Lines representing the direction of the detail from the instrument are drawn on the paper using the side of the alidade. The distances to the detail can be measured by tape (or by tacheometry if a telescopic alidade is used) and the scale distances plotted on the board. An example of the radiation method is shown in Figure 3.9.

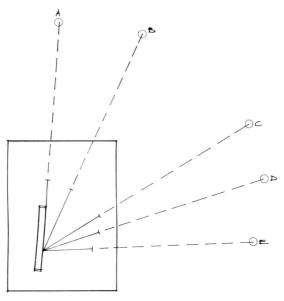

Figure 3.9 Radiation.

♦ *Intersection.* A baseline is set up and measured. Points of detail are located by two sightings, one from each end of the baseline. This method avoids having to measure the distance from the plane-table to the points observed. An example of this method is shown in Figure 3.10.

♦ *Traversing.* Traversing is a method of surveying in which a control framework is formed by straight lines, the length of each line and the angle between successive lines being measured. An example is shown in Figure 3.11.

The plane-table is set up at each survey station in turn and sightings made on forward and back stations. The distance between each station is taped.

A closed-loop traverse, which fails to close because of inaccurate observations or measurements, may be adjusted using the method described below.

In Figure 3.12 a closing error of $A-A_1$ is indicated. To adjust this, the individual lines making up the traverse are drawn out as a continuous straight line $ABCDEA_1$. At A_1 on this line, a perpendicular $A-A_2$ is erected and scaled to a length equal to the closing error. A_2 is joined to A, and perpendiculars cutting A_2A are erected from points B, C, D and E. The perpendiculars show the proportionate amount of error to be allowed for at each angle of the traverse. On the original survey, plotting lines are drawn parallel to the misclosure $A-A_1$, and by marking off on these parallels the respective proportions of error as determined above,

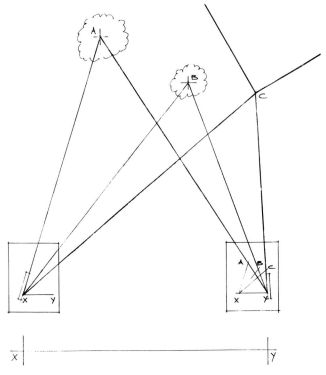

Figure 3.10 Intersecting.

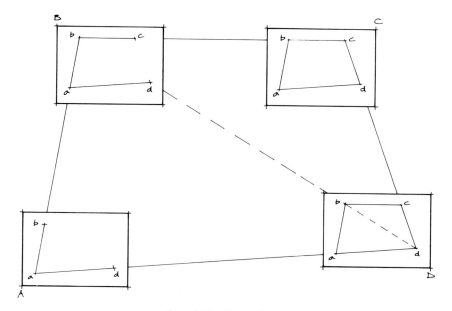

Figure 3.11 Traversing.

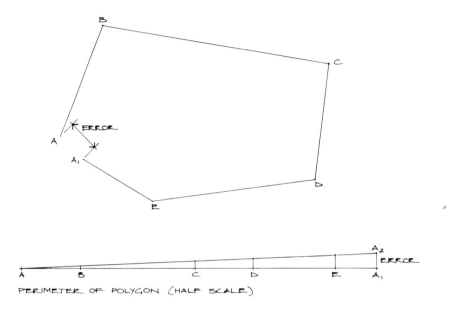

PERIMETER OF POLYGON (HALF SCALE)

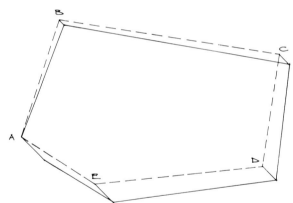

Figure 3.12   Corretion of traverse closing errors.

and by joining the points so obtained, the traverse is replotted and will now close (Figure 3.12).

The chief advantages of the plane-table survey are:

1. The equipment is inexpensive and easy to use.
2. No computation is necessary, and all the plotting is carried out in the field thereby reducing the chances of omitting details.
3. Field-notes are kept to a minimum and booking errors eliminated.

CHECKLIST OF FEATURES TO BE RECORDED ON A MEASURED SITE SURVEY

♦ Access roads – name, classification, width, metalled/unmetalled.
♦ Boundaries – position; how defined, e.g. hedge, ditch, wall, fence; width or thickness.
♦ Rights of way across the site; footpaths, bridleways.
♦ Positions of gates and stiles.
♦ Hedgerows.
♦ Trees – girth, spread, species.
♦ Ditches, ponds, watercourses and associated features, e.g. sluices, lock gates, landing stages, slipways.
♦ Bridges, viaducts, aqueducts and causeways – width, headroom, weight restrictions.
♦ Tunnels and ventilation shafts.
♦ Cuttings and embankments.
♦ Quarries and mineral workings.
♦ Ruins and evidence of former occupation and land use.
♦ Buildings on the site and immediately adjacent to the site boundaries together with their associated outbuildings.
♦ Features associated with buildings, e.g. paved areas, railings, steps, gate piers, pumps, troughs.
♦ Features of planned landscapes, e.g. terraces, ha-has, grottoes, temples, follies, gazebos, mausoleums, triumphal arches, fountains, statues, urns and obelisks.
♦ Services – positions of manhole and access covers, gullies, hydrants, lamp standards, electricity and telegraph poles, overhead lines (including a note of the clearance or headroom available).

CHAPTER FOUR

Levelling

Levelling is concerned with determining the heights of features on the surface of the earth relative to a known datum. With the data produced from a levelling survey, gradients can be computed and contours drawn on plans.

PRINCIPLES OF LEVELLING

1. A surveyor's level is set up on a tripod (refer to Chapter 2 for details of levels and setting up procedures). Before making any observations the instrument must be adjusted for the surveyor's eye so that the cross-hairs are correctly focused. This is done by pointing the telescope at a light background and turning the eyepiece until the cross-hairs appear black and sharply in focus. Once this adjustment has been made the surveyor does not need to make any further corrections to the eyepiece unless the setting is accidentally disturbed.

2. With the level correctly set up, the surveyor's line of sight along the centreline of the telescope is horizontal. The line of sight is referred to as the *line of collimation*, and the relative heights of points of detail are determined by reference to measurements taken above or below this line. The surveyor sights onto a levelling staff, placed on each point of detail in turn, and notes the reading on the staff where it is cut by the central cross-hair, which represents the difference in height between the line of collimation and the point of detail.

Most modern instruments have a telescope which gives an erect image, that is the objects appear the right way up. However, some older

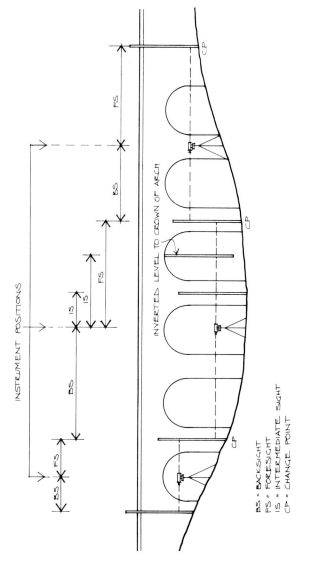

INSTRUMENT POSITIONS

BS = BACKSIGHT
FS = FORESIGHT
IS = INTERMEDIATE SIGHT
CP = CHANGE POINT

Figure 4.1 Levelling.

instruments may still be encountered which provide an inverted image, and these require a little practice when taking the reading from the staff as it will appear upside-down in the eyepiece.

Normally, readings are taken to points of detail below the line of collimation, but there are occasions when *inverted staff* readings are taken to details above the collimation line, for instance the underside of a bridge.

3. Readings can be taken to several points of detail from one instrument position if it is carefully chosen. However, for most surveys it will be necessary to move the instrument several times in order to cover all the points of detail required. Whenever the level has to be repositioned, the staff must remain on the last point of detail, so that a second reading onto that point can be made from the new instrument position before fresh points of detail are observed. The reason for this procedure at a *change point* is so that the difference in height between the old and the new collimation lines can be measured.

4. The first reading to be taken in a series of levels is referred to as a *backsight*. Subsequent readings from the same instrument position are called *intermediate sights*. The last reading to be taken before moving the instrument is called a *foresight*. The next reading from the new instrument position is a *backsight* and so on. Figure 4.1 shows a levelling task requiring backsight, intermediate sight and foresight readings.

Equipment

The basic equipment for a levelling survey comprises:

> Optical level (dumpy, tilting or automatic)
> Tripod for the level
> Levelling staff
> Change plate (for use on soft ground at a change point)
> Star for the tripod (on hard, slippery surfaces)
> Level book

SURVEY PROCEDURE

1. The levelling survey team consists of the surveyor, who stays with the instrument and books the readings, and an assistant or *staffholder*, who moves the staff from point to point under the direction of the surveyor.

2. With the level set up, the first reading, or backsight, is generally taken to the staff held on an Ordnance Survey bench-mark (OSBM). OSBMs are marked points whose height is known with respect to mean sea level at Newlyn in Cornwall. The positions and heights of OSBMs are marked on 1:1250 and 1:2500 Ordnance Survey maps. The most common type of

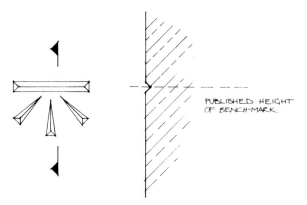

Figure 4.2   Cut Ordnance Survey bench-mark.

OSBM is a cut bench-mark, in the form of a broad arrow, cut into the brickwork or stonework of buildings and boundary walls (Figure 4.2).

In the absence of a convenient OSBM, a temporary bench-mark (TBM) is used. This may be any permanent feature which can be easily found again, such as the corner of a manhole cover. The TBM is given an arbitary level, say 100.000 m. If necessary, a series of *flying levels*, that is levelling without any intermediate levels, may be made from the TBM to the nearest OSBM and an absolute value above sea level computed for the TBM.

It is important that the staffholder keeps the staff vertical when each reading is taken, and for this a staff bubble may be found useful.

3. The staffholder is directed to various points of detail, and staff readings for each of these booked as intermediate sights. Communication between the surveyor and the assistant frequently has to be by hand signals as the distances between them is too great for verbal instructions, unless portable radio handsets are used. Appendix A contains details of commonly used hand signals.

4. When a change point is necessary, the point chosen should be one where the distance of the backsight from the new instrument position to the staff should be approximately equal to the distance of the foresight from the old instrument position. The purpose of keeping foresights and backsights as equal as possible is to reduce the risk of errors due to refraction or collimation accumulating. An experienced staffholder will remember the number of paces from the instrument for the foresight, and communicate this information to the surveyor for use when moving the instrument to a new position.

5. It is good practice to close a series of levels onto the bench-mark chosen for the first reading. Some misclosure may be expected, but for general site surveying the following limit should not be exceeded:

$5\sqrt{s}$ mm

where s = the number of instrument set-ups used.

Level survey booking procedures

During a levelling survey the backsights, intermediate sights and foresights are noted in a ruled level book. Two forms of level book are available, the choice depending on the method preferred by the surveyor to *reduce* or calculate the levels. The two calculation methods are *rise and fall* and *collimation height*. Both methods of calculation and their associated level books are described by reference to a practical example.

In our example, the level is set up in a dockyard and the first observation, a backsight, is made onto an OSBM cut into the wall of an industrial mill building. From the same instrument position intermediate sights are taken to determine the levels of the wharf, water in the basin, and the road surface and soffit of a swing bridge. The last reading from the first instrument position is to a weighbridge, which acts as a *change point* (CP), and is therefore booked as a foresight and then booked again from the second instrument position as a backsight (as both readings refer to the same point they are booked on the same line). The intention of the surveyor is to close the survey on an OSBM on the wall of the Jolly Higglers public house in Dock Road, but this is separated from the dockyard by a high wall. The top of this wall is used as a CP, and to obtain a reading the staff has to be *inverted*. The staff is turned upside-down and the base of the staff held level with the top of the wall, the reading taken being booked as a minus value. The surveyor and staffholder pass through the wall via the dockyard gate to emerge on Dock Road, where a new instrument position is selected opposite the point where the last staff reading was taken. The staffholder inverts the staff on the Dock Road side of the wall and holds it level with the top at a position directly opposite that where the last (foresight) reading was taken. The next reading (booked as a backsight), being onto an inverted staff, is also booked as a minus value. The last reading onto the OSBM is booked as a foresight.

Rise and fall method

Once the observations have been booked into their respective column (Table 4.1) the surveyor reduces the levels as follows:

1. The level at the OSBM on Kett's Mill is taken from the 1 : 2500 OS sheet for the area. If a TBM had been used, a notional value, of say 100.000 m, would have been adopted to represent its height above sea level.

Table 4.1   Rise and fall method of booking

Back-sight	Intermediate	Foresight	Rise	Fall	Reduced level	Remarks
1.736					47.340	OSBM corner of Kett's Mill
	3.009			1.273	46.067	Wharf next to boat crane
	3.457			0.448	45.619	Water level in basin
	2.682		0.775		46.394	Road deck of swing bridge
	3.007			0.325	46.069	U/S of swing bridge
1.532		3.261		0.254	45.815	CP1 Coal Yard weightbridge
−3.748		−3.624	5.156		50.971	CP2 top of wall to Dock Rd
		1.229		4.977	45.994	OSBM Jolly Higglers PH
						45.99 AOD
−0.480		0.866	5.931	7.277	47.340	
−0.866			−7.277			
−1.346			−1.346		−1.346	

2. The rises (positive values) and falls (negative values) are calculated by subtracting each observation from the previous one.

$$
\begin{array}{lll}
1.736 - 3.009 & = & -1.273 \quad \text{fall} \\
3.009 - 3.457 & = & -0.446 \quad \text{fall} \\
3.457 - 2.682 & = & +0.775 \quad \text{rise} \\
2.682 - 3.007 & = & -0.325 \quad \text{fall} \\
3.007 - 3.261 & = & -0.254 \quad \text{fall} \\
1.532 - (-3.624) & = & +5.156 \quad \text{rise} \\
-3.748 - 1.229 & = & -4.977 \quad \text{fall}
\end{array}
$$

3. The sum of the backsights minus the sum of the foresights should equal the sum of the rises minus the sum of the falls.
4. If the arithmetic is correct, the level for each point of detail is computed by adding the rises or subtracting the falls from the reduced level of the previously observed point. As a further arithmetical check, the last reduced level minus the first reduced level should be equal to the value computed in the previous check.
5. The checks described in 3 and 4 apply to the arithmetic only, they do not check the accuracy of the observations. A check on accuracy can be made either by closing on the first point observed, or by using starting and finishing points whose relative heights to a selected datum are known. In the example there is a misclosure of 4 mm between the reduced level and the known height of the bench-mark on the last observation. The permissible misclosure is $5\sqrt{s}$ mm or $5\sqrt{3} = 8.6$ mm, so the error is acceptable. If required, closing errors can be distributed uniformly throughout the levelling by applying a correction at each CP:

47.340
46.067
45.619
46.394
46.069
45.815 − 0.002 = 45.813
45.813 + 5.156 − 0.002 = 50.967
50.967 − 4.977 = 45.99

Collimation height method

Once the observations have been booked into their respective column (Table 4.2) the surveyor reduces the levels as follows:

1. The first backsight is added to the level of the OSBM on Kett's Mill to give the height of the instrument or collimation height.
2. Each intermediate sight is deducted from the collimation height (or added to it if it is an inverted staff reading) to give the reduced level.
3. At a CP a new collimation height is computed by adding the new backsight to the calculated reduced level for that point.
4. As an arithmetical check, the sum of the backsights minus the sum of the foresights should equal the last reduced level minus the first reduced level.

Of the two booking methods, experienced surveyors prefer the height of collimation level procedure as it is quicker to use. Beginners are recommended to use the rise and fall method as this has more arithmetical checks on the computation.

Table 4.2 Collimation height method of booking

Back-sight	Intermediate	Foresight	Collimation	Reduced level	Remarks
1.736			49,076	47.340	OSBM corner of Kett's Mill
	3.009			46.067	Wharf next to boat crane
	3.457			45.619	Water level in basin
	2.682			46.394	Road deck of swing bridge
	3.007			46.069	U/S of swing bridge
1.532		3.261	47.347	45.815	CP1 Coal Yard weighbridge
−3.748		−3,624	47.223	50.971	CP2 top of wall to Dock Rd
		1.229		45.994	OSBM Jolly Higglers PH
					45.99 AOD
−0.480		−0.866		47.340	
−0.866				−1.346	
−1.346					

When reducing levels, by whichever method, it is best to check each page separately, so space should be left at the bottom of each page for this purpose. During booking, when the bottom of a page is reached, the last reading to be recorded on that page should be booked as a foresight and then rebooked at the top of the next page in the level book, this time as a backsight.

CONTOURING

Contour lines, that is lines on a map or plan that join up all points of equal height above a chosen datum, can convey more readily the topography of a piece of land than spot heights alone. In order to enable contours to be plotted, a regular grid of levels is required over the land concerned. Typically, ten- or twenty-metre grids are used, depending on the level of detail required.

Equipment for grid levelling

The basic equipment is as for a levelling survey, together with the following items:

> Ranging rods
> Optical square
> Chain
> Tape
> Chaining arrows

Procedure for grid levelling

1. A suitable baseline is selected and its ends marked with ranging rods, which are then tied in by measurements to the survey control framework.
2. Using a chain or tape, chaining arrows are positioned at the selected grid interval along the baseline.
3. An offset is raised at each grid interval and lines set out at right angles to the baseline, and using the chain the grid interval positions marked with chaining arrows.
4. For a large grid, time and labour can be saved if a double row of ranging rods is set along the baseline and one adjacent side at the required grid intervals (Figure 4.3). The staffholder can then find the other grid positions by lining in with pairs of ranging rods.
5. Levels are taken at each grid intersection. In booking the observations, a system of reference letters along one axis and numbers along the other is employed to identify the individual intersection points.

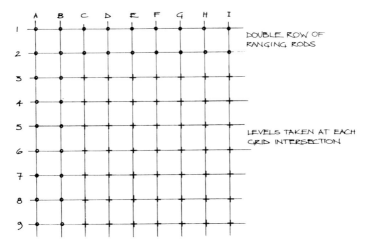

Figure 4.3 Grid layout.

Procedure for drawing contours

1. The grid is plotted in pencil on cartridge paper, and the reduced level for each intersection point noted adjacent to the point referred to.
2. A suitable *contour interval*, being the difference in height between successive contours, is selected. Suitable intervals might be 0.2 m or 0.5 m.
3. Each contour line is plotted by interpolating between the spot heights at the grid intersection points. This takes a little practice, and it is best to start with either the highest or lowest point on the site and work systematically, contour by contour, over the site.
4. The contour lines, when finalized, can be traced onto the finished survey drawing.

Figure 4.4 shows an example of contouring.

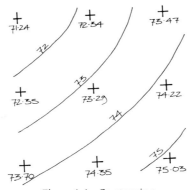

Figure 4.4 Contouring.

CHAPTER FIVE

Building Surveys I: Preliminaries and Sketching

In order to carry out a competent measured survey of a building the surveyor should:

1. Have a knowledge of the basic principles of surveying and levelling as described in the foregoing chapters.
2. Be familiar with the techniques and materials used in the construction of buildings and their associated services.
3. Be observant, especially if the survey is an analytical one to record, say, the various phases in the development of a historic building, or its structural arrangement, including evidence of movement and distortions.

Before any measurements are taken, the surveyor must undertake a certain amount of preparatory work to ensure that the objectives of the survey will be met, and that the survey will be conducted in a safe and efficient manner.

SAFETY

In surveying, as in any other occupation, safe working practices should always be adopted, especially in unoccupied and derelict buildings or when working alone. The following notes are offered as guidance for good practice.

Clothing

Wear sensible and comfortable clothing that will keep you warm and dry. Overalls and a stout pair of shoes are advisable. In derelict buildings, a safety helmet and safety boots or shoes with steel toe-caps should be worn. Have rubber gloves available if you expect to lift drainage inspection covers.

Working alone

Make sure someone knows where you are, when to expect you back, and what action to take if you do not return when anticipated. If your plans change, keep your contact informed.

Check empty buildings thoroughly for unauthorized occupants. Discarded syringes, empty cider, wine and spirits bottles should put you on caution. If persons are found, who may be hostile, consideration of a planned escape route may be prudent. It might be wise to carry a personal alarm.

If the building is definitely empty and no signs of recent occupation are visible, close external doors when working internally and either lock them (making sure you have the keys readily to hand) or place a chair or similar object against them which will make a noise if the door is opened, so giving advance warning of intruders.

Unoccupied buildings

Buildings that have been empty and shut up for some time may prove to be dangerous as a result of deterioration, vandalism, or both. Before starting your survey, examine the building carefully for hazards such as rotten floor-boards, upstanding nails, joists and staircases that will not support your weight; unguarded openings in floors; bare electrical cables that are live; sharp protruding pipes; bulging, leaning or loose masonry, and balconies with corroded support brackets.

Health hazards

Buildings, especially empty ones, and their contents may be contaminated. A building may be infested with vermin, and dirty soft furnishings may harbour flees and lice. Cuts, even minor ones, should be attended to promptly: an open wound can easily become infected. Surveyors should always carry a basic first aid kit and know how to use it. Buildings that pose particular health risks are those that have housed livestock (tetanous), or are infested with vermin (Weil's disease). There is even a health risk from dead birds – pigeon fancier's lung – caused by fungal spores on the corpse.

Cleanliness is a good first line of defence against infection, so ensure that you will have access to soap, towel and water and be able to wash, particularly before eating or drinking any refreshments.

Wearing a face mask is prudent in dusty atmospheres. Particularly hazardous is asbestos, which may be present as insulation around heating pipes and in other locations. If loose asbestos fibres are suspected, abandon the survey until a check has been made by a competent testing organization to ascertain whether the limits given in the Health and Safety Executive's guidance note E10 have been exceeded.

Be vigilant for, and avoid disturbing, the nests of stinging insects such as wasps which are sometimes found in roof spaces.

If you become ill, consider the possibility of the illness being due to your work, and give your doctor information of any risks you think you may have been exposed to.

BRIEFING

At the briefing stage it is important to establish the purpose of the survey and its extent, as very detailed surveys are time consuming and therefore expensive. There is no point in measuring to a greater level of detail than is needed. If necessary, greater detail could be added to a basic survey at a later date, so working from the whole to the part. Under no circumstances should accuracy be compromised in an attempt to reduce costs. It is far better to have an accurate survey, showing only a basic level of detail, than one showing more detail, but whose accuracy cannot be guaranteed.

Establish with the client the following points:

1. The extent to which services are to be recorded. Generally speaking, measurements are always taken so that service intake positions, sanitary fittings, cylinders, cisterns, tanks, boilers, soil and vent pipes, rainwater pipes, below-ground drainage with associated gullies, and inspection chambers can be plotted. Any additional information that the client may require, such as the position of radiators, socket outlets, lighting points and invert levels should be established.
2. The level of detail to be shown on the elevations. Normally, all openings in walls and their associated surrounds, quoins, label moulds, exposed timber framing, plinths, string courses, cornices, pilasters, engaged columns, niches, parapets, balustrades, shaped gables, copings, finials, pinnacles, bellcotes, porches, steps, railings and external pipework are recorded, as are rooflines including, ridges and hips, chimney stacks, dormer windows, skylights, lanterns, flêches, and cupolas. If additional details, including a stone-by-stone survey, detailed measurement of

statuary, strapwork, pargetting or other applied ornament, are required, then these should be clearly specified.

3. The level of detail that is required internally. Usually, the positions of walls, openings in walls, door swings, staircases, fireplaces, exposed joists, beams, and the direction of floor-boards are recorded. Additional details, such as internal elevations to show panelling, architraves, skirtings, dados, friezes, fireplace surrounds and ceiling plans to show plasterwork may sometimes be required.
4. Whether detailed profiles will be required of timber, stone or plaster mouldings and other enrichments.

The more extensive the detail required, the greater the time and effort that will have to be spent, both on site taking the measurements, and in the office plotting the survey and preparing the finished drawings. The level of detail required will be an important determinant in costing a job for tendering purposes.

RECONNAISSANCE

It is advisable to visit the building to be surveyed prior to the survey proper in order to view the premises and to carry out the following preliminaries:

1. To establish the nature and complexity of the job.
2. To plan out a strategy for conducting the survey. For instance, a large building might be best tackled by carrying out the work in phases, the first phase being a control survey to establish the overall layout and geometry of each floor, together with the levels of floors and landings; subsequent phases measure in detail, and are tied back to control survey of the first phase.
3. To check to see if all parts of the building are safely accessible or whether additional facilities will need to be provided, including long ladders, scaffolding or hydraulic platforms.
4. To check on the availability of electrical lighting, sanitation and, occasionally, heating.
5. To assess the resources needed in terms of personnel, equipment and time.
6. Collect sufficient information upon which to base a tender for the work.

PRELIMINARIES TO A SURVEY

Equipment

The basic surveying equipment for a measured building survey is:

Thirty-metre tape
Two-metre surveyor's rod
Five-metre steel pocket tape with blade lock
A3 clipboard and paper
Pencils (preferably fineline retractables, including spare leads)
Fine-tipped fibre pens of various colours
Chalk
Draughting tape
Plumb-bob and string
Spirit level
Magnetic compass
Handlamp (plus spare bulb and batteries)
Portfolio or plastic wallets to store paper and completed notes

In addition to the above, the following equipment is desirable:

Level and levelling staff
Camera, tripod and flash to record complex detail and ornament
Four-metre surveyors' sectional ladder
Vernier calipers and profile gauge for measuring mould profiles
Manhole keys

Preparatory work

1. Collect any extant drawn survey information. Possible sources include the owners or their professional advisors, such as solicitors and land agents; drawings deposited with local authorities for building control or planning purposes in the past; archive material held by County Record Offices, local history and civic societies. All drawn material so collected should be treated with some degree of caution as drawings may show designs that were subsequently modified on site, or buildings before extensions or adaptations took place, and, of course, they may be of dubious accuracy. No survey drawing should be taken on trust, it should be checked carefully against the building itself before any reliance is placed on it.

   Old drawings, even if somewhat inaccurate, are, nonetheless, useful if they are reproduced, or even enlarged, on a photocopier, to provide sheet(s) upon which measured information can be booked on site.
2. Obtain a photocopied extract from a large-scale Ordnance Survey sheet (1:1250 or 1:2500 scale) showing the building, its site and immediate environs.
3. Make arrangements for access (keys and ladders), and gain the permission of third parties if you will need to enter their land or premises to complete your survey.

4. Assemble the surveying equipment and check that it is serviceable.
5. Brief an assistant. Measurement is best carried out by a surveyor and an assistant, as single-handed surveying is often inefficient and tends to be inaccurate.

SURVEY PROCEDURE: PREPARING SKETCHES

Before any measurement can take place sketch plans, sections and elevations must be prepared of all parts of the subject building. The surveyor might tackle this work alone, and only bring an assistant when the measurement starts, or if a competent assistant is available, divide the sketching work between the two of them.

1. Using plain paper securely clipped to an A3 board, of either plywood or hardboard, produce a key reference sketch plan of the building. Initially the sketch should be drawn lightly in pencil, a 0.5 mm fine retractable with HB leads being suitable for most surveyors.

In order to keep the sketch roughly in proportion and produce a fair representation of the plan shape, some surveyors use an underlay of graph paper and gauge the length of individual walls by pacing. A sonic tape could be used for the same purpose, but should not be relied upon for accurate measurement. When satisfied with the sketch it may be 'firmed up' in pencil or felt tip pen.

The following information should be shown on the key reference sketch:

♦ A north point (use a compass or take from an OS sheet).
♦ The arrangement of the roof slopes, positions of stacks and dormer windows.
♦ A reference letter at each corner of the building so that every length of external wall can be identified by a two-letter code.
♦ Notes indicating the number of storeys, approximate age, and materials used for each part of the building.
♦ Name of the job, surveyor(s) responsible, and the date(s) of the survey.
♦ A sheet number ('sheet one of . . .'). Subsequent sheets should be numbered consecutively, bear the job name, and state the contents. At the end of the survey, the total number of sheets used should be noted on each individual sheet.

A key reference plan is shown in Figure 5.1.

2. Starting with the ground floor, draw out a floor plan for each floor level in the building. In preparing floor plans the following principles should be observed:

♦ The plan should be drawn as a plane that is notionally at breast height (as

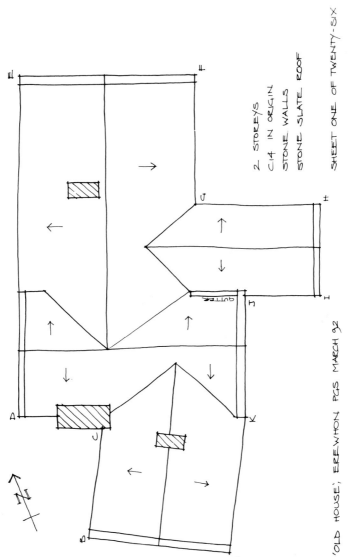

Figure 5.1 A key reference plan.

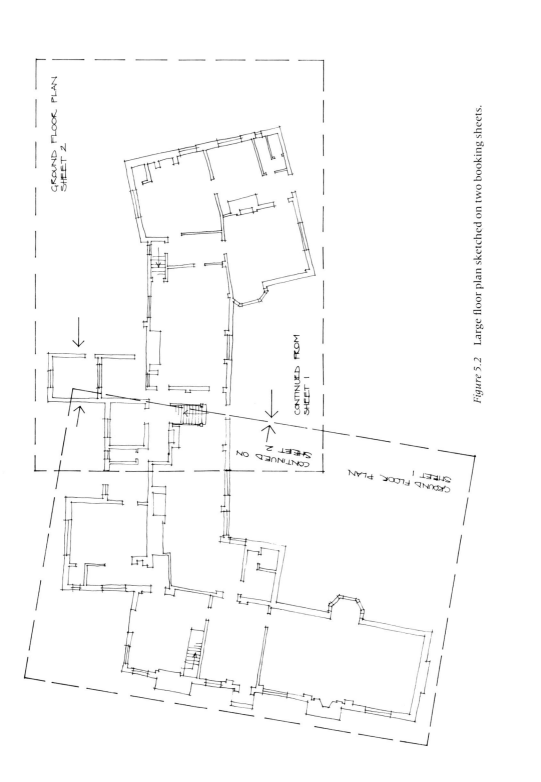

Figure 5.2   Large floor plan sketched on two booking sheets.

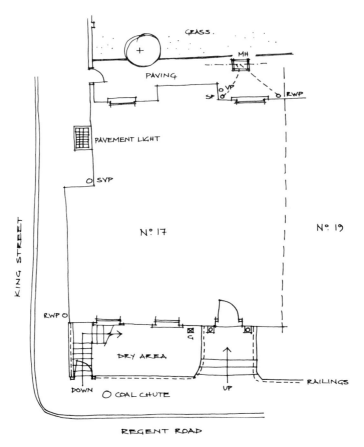

Figure 5.3(a) Ground floor plan. Stage 1 sketched externally.

measurements are conveniently taken at this height); features below the plane are indicated with a solid line and those above with a broken line.

♦ If at all possible, draw out the complete ground floor plan onto a single booking sheet. For large buildings this may not be feasible and the building must be broken up into convenient blocks for measurement and booking purposes. If a floor level is recorded on more than one booking sheet, care must be taken to reference the booking sheets to each other and to ensure that sufficient measurements are taken so that their contents will tie together when plotted (an example is shown in Figure 5.2).

♦ In order to keep the ground floor plan roughly in proportion, it is best to start from the outside by drawing the perimeter. Taking each wall length in turn, the following detail is recorded: projections and setbacks, door and window openings, dry areas, external steps, railings, pavement

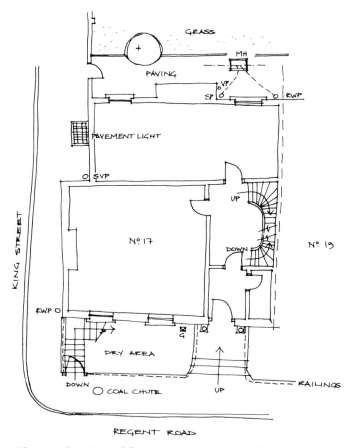

Figure 5.3(b)   Ground floor plan. Stage 2 internal layout added.

lights, gratings, gullies, soil pipes, vent pipes and rainwater pipes. Additionally, if the survey is an analytical one, changes in material, straight joints and blocked openings are noted. Figure 5.3 shows a floor plan drawn up in two stages.

♦ With the perimeter completed, the internal arrangement of the ground floor can be added. It is best to start with the largest rooms around the perimeter first, and get a feel for the main walls in the building, before moving onto corridors, lobbies and minor rooms. Work methodically on a room-by-room basis (occasionally it may be necessary to refer to adjacent rooms to establish details of planning arrangements that may not be entirely clear from one side only). Distinguish between load-bearing walls and non-load-bearing partitions and show their relative thicknesses.

♦ It is generally best to establish the overall plan arrangement before adding detail. Once a satisfactory plan has been drawn in outline, the following detail should be added: reveals to openings, which may be

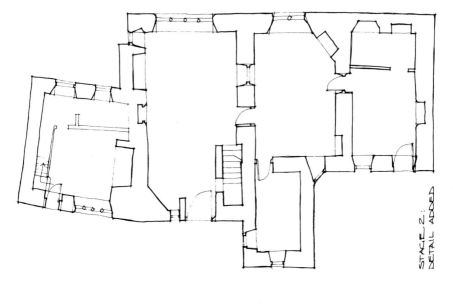

STAGE 2:
DETAIL ADDED

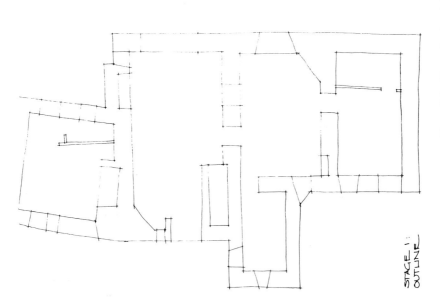

STAGE 1:
OUTLINE

Figure 5.4   Stages in sketching a ground floor plan – example no. 2.

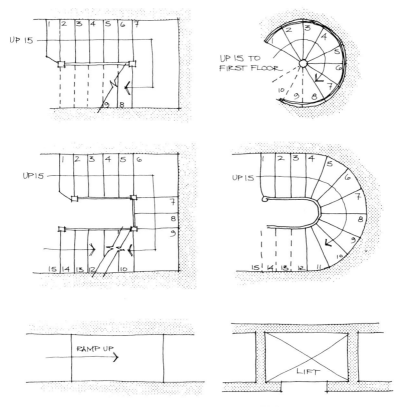

Figure 5.5 Stairs, ramps and lifts.

square or splayed; door swings, plant (such as boilers and air con-
ditioning units), sanitary and other fittings. The positions of overhead
features such as beams, trusses and rooflights should be indicated using
a broken line. A second example of the compilation of a floor plan is
shown in Figure 5.4.

♦ Stairs and stairwells must be drawn carefully and show the positions of
risers and landings, using broken lines to show hidden construction or
steps above plan level. Each riser should be numbered consecutively
starting from the bottom of the flight. Changes in level, whether
isolated steps, flights of stairs or ramps, should be indicated with an
arrow labelled 'up' or 'down' as appropriate (Figure 5.5).

♦ Any detail which is too intricate to be shown at the scale of the floor
plan can be amplified by a larger sketch drawn in the margin. The
position of the detail and the sketch should be given a unique reference
code, perhaps using a lower-case letter.

♦ Note the direction of the floor boards of suspended timber floors – joists
will normally run at right angles to them, unless the existing boards

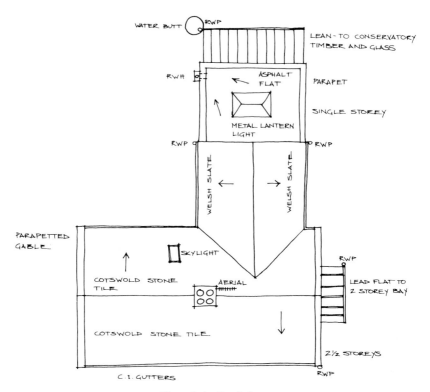

Figure 5.6 Roof plan.

Figure 5.7 Section.

have become worn and been overlaid with boarding laid at right angles to the original boards. The centres of the joists may be determined by measuring between successive rows of floor brads.

Note the various wall, floor and ceiling finishes in each room. In order to save time and space, abbreviations may be used. Appendix B contains a useful list of commonly used abbreviations.

Plans for the remaining floors, if any, can often be conveniently prepared by tracing the main lines of external walls, internal walls, stairwells, and chimney breasts from the ground floor plan onto detail or tracing paper. These plans are then worked up as described above.

3. If the exterior of the roof is accessible, for example via a hatch, draw out a roof plan and show the following features: roof pitches with the direction of the slope and all associated hips, valleys and ridges; flat roofs including falls, rolls and drips as appropriate; parapets and associated gutters; valley gutters, boundary gutters and eaves gutters, rainwater heads and outlets; dormer windows, rooflights and skylights; chimney stacks; plant and plant rooms; lightning protection systems, aerials, satellite and communications dishes. Note the various materials used. A roof plan is shown in Figure 5.6.

4. Draw out sections through the building at points that will convey the maximum amount of information. Typically, the following details are conveniently shown on a section:

◆ The shape and arrangement of the structural timbers in pitched roofs.
◆ The relative levels of the various floors in the building together with the floor thicknesses and depths of beams.
◆ The relationship of ground and basement floors to external ground level(s).
◆ Staircases including headroom under landings.
◆ Heights of ceilings, door and window heads, sill heights.

An example of a section is given in Figure 5.7.

5. Draw out elevations for each face of the building, referencing them to code letters on the key plan. In drawing out an elevation, it is best to stand some distance back at a position where the outline and shape can be clearly seen and the proportions best judged. The first line to draw is the eaves line, which is shown horizontal, followed by a vertical line representing the wall on the extreme left. The vertical representing extreme right of the wall is drawn next. The position of the ground is marked off at each end of the building and the ground line drawn (which may be at a slope). Next, other vertical axes can be drawn followed by the main horizontal divisions. Detail is then filled in on this framework (Figure 5.8).

As an aid to judging proportion, a scale rule can be held at arm's length

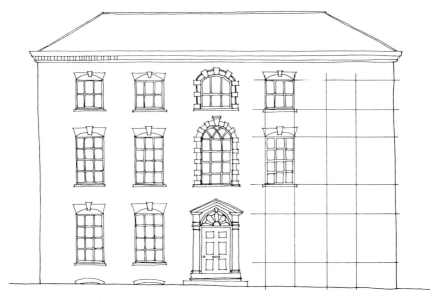

FRAMEWORK OF HORIZONTAL AND
VERTICAL LINES TO IDENTIFY
OPENING TO WHICH DETAIL IS
ADDED

Figure 5.8   Sketching an elevation.

with the zero mark aligned with one end of a feature. By moving the
thumb up or down the rule until it is in line with the other end, the relative
height to width ratios can be determined by reference to the number of
graduations read off the rule for each feature.

The following features should be shown on the drawing:

♦ Window and door openings, together with associated construction
(arches, lintels, surrounds, sub-sills, canopies, porches and steps).
♦ Door-frames and doors, including fanlights, sidelights, details of panelling and ornamental features.
♦ Window-frames including transomes, mullions, opening lights and
glazing bars. Only one of each type of window need be detailed
thoroughly and given a reference code, say W/a (window type *a*); where
the same type of window occurs again annotate the drawing W/a.
♦ Plinth and string courses, rustication, recessed panels, pilasters, engaged
columns, blind arcading and other decorative features.
♦ Rainwater goods and sanitary pipework.
♦ Roof, chimney stacks and other associated construction.

Note the materials and finishes used.

CHAPTER SIX

Building Surveys II: Measuring

Once the plans, sections and elevations of the building to be surveyed have been sketched out the process of measuring can begin. It is usual to measure in the following order: plans, sections and then elevations. However, there are no hard-and-fast rules about this, the order can be changed to suit the circumstances or the preferences of the surveyor concerned. What is important is that measurement is carried out in a methodical and orderly way so that nothing is missed and the survey can be plotted from notes efficiently and without ambiguity.

MEASURING FOR PLANS

Generally speaking, most of the measurement is carried out using a thirty metre woven tape, but in confined spaces a steel pocket tape may be more convenient. Most surveyors begin by measuring internally, the surveying of the exterior on plan is generally combined with the measurement of the elevations.

Wherever possible, linear measurements should be taken as *running dimensions* rather than a series of separate measurements to successive points of detail. This procedure reduces cumulative error, as each individual dimension will usually be rounded up or down to the nearest ten millimetres (when plotting to a scale of 1:50). Taking running dimensions is also a quicker procedure when working with an assistant in the field, and it also facilitates rapid and more accurate plotting.

In taking the measurements, it is usual for the surveyor to hold the ring or zero end of the tape, and book the dimensions called out by the assistant as the points of detail are measured in. To reduce the risk of booking a misheard dimension, the surveyor should repeat the dimension, which if correct will signal the assistant to move onto the next point of detail. It is important that the assistant is well briefed about the details to be measured and the accuracy required.

The following points should be noted:

1. The tape should be held taut at about breast height.
2. Projections and recesses are most conveniently measured as they are encountered by the assistant, using a rod or pocket tape.
3. Where window openings occur, the structural opening is measured.
4. Doorways are measured to the structural opening if it is visible, but if masked by architraves measure to the edges of the linings and note this on the sketch.
5. Measure wall thicknesses at window and door openings (Figure 6.1). In the case of the latter, appropriate allowance must be made for projecting linings and architraves.
6. If the wall being measured exceeds the tape length, the thirty metre point can be marked on the wall surface in pencil, or on a piece of draughting tape, which can easily be seen by the surveyor moving up to the new position, and be removed without damage to the building fabric when its purpose has been served.
7. Sufficient measurements must be taken in each room to ensure its

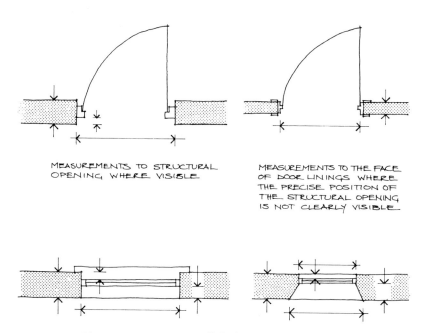

Figure 6.1 Measuring wall thicknesses and openings.

shape can be plotted. For a simple rectangular room, this means taking the length of each wall together with diagonal measurements corner-to-corner (both diagonals are taken, although only one is needed for plotting, the other acts as a check). Where rooms or spaces in a building are non-rectangular, or irregular in plan form, sufficient diagonals or tie dimensions must be taken to ensure that the shape can be recorded accurately, and the geometry of the plot checked. Never assume that apparently square corners are in fact exactly 90 degrees.

8. Measurements must be booked in a clear and unambiguous way. Space for writing down the dimensions is often quite limited, so the surveyor must cultivate the ability to book figures down in a small, neat hand. A fine-point felt-tipped pen is useful for booking down, except in damp conditions when a pencil is the only reliable medium that will not run. Two approaches are possible when booking down dimensions (Figure 6.2):

   ♦ Book the dimensions against dimension lines. This method may be the safest for beginners, but the dimension lines may congest and confuse the sketch. The use of different colours for the sketch and the dimension lines might be helpful to distinguish between the two.

   ♦ Book the dimensions with the figures written the correct way up for reading when the field-notes are orientated with features being recorded, and the surveyor is facing the direction in which the dimensions are being taken. This method requires a little practice, but it is generally preferred by experienced surveyors, as it is quicker and leaves the field notes less cluttered.

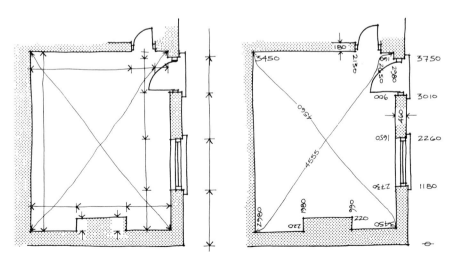

Figure 6.2   Booking dimensions on plan.

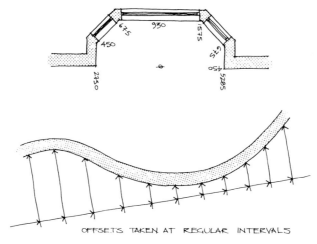

OFFSETS TAKEN AT REGULAR INTERVALS

Figure 6.3 Measuring bays and meandering walls.

Use a zero mark if the starting point for the first dimension is not entirely clear. Diagonals and ties are booked with the base of the figures on the measured line.

9. Straight-sided bays, curved and meandering walls may be measured by taking offsets as illustrated in Figure 6.3.

10. At every opportunity take running dimensions through as many internal spaces as door openings will allow. These long dimensions will be useful during the plotting process and are invaluable in tying the survey together accurately (Figure 6.4).

11. Where staircases occur, measure to establish the flight width, and the position of the risers at the top and bottom of flights and landings.

MEASURING FOR SECTIONS

Heighting information to enable sections to be constructed accurately may be collected using a tape and rod alone, or in conjunction with a levelling survey using an optical level and staff.

The relative levels of floors and landings in a building are most accurately determined by using a surveyor's level and staff. The method of using the level and booking the information has been covered in Chapter 4, but the following additional points should be noted:

1. Establish a TBM, say on the threshold of the principal entrance to the building, and start and end the survey at this point.

2. It is usual to take levels to determine floor, landing and floor soffit levels only. Heights to ceilings, sills and to the heads of openings, are usually taken by tape and rod using the floor as a datum.

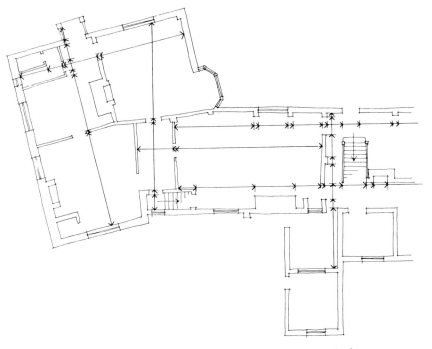

Figure 6.4 Running dimensions through internal spaces to tie the survey together.

3. Levelling up staircases, especially narrow ones, can be awkward, as the instrument at change points may need to be set up on a landing or even in mid-flight. For preference, an automatic level should be used as it is easier to set up. Great care must be taken by both surveyor and staffholder not to disturb the level as they change positions and move around the instrument. Inverted staff readings are frequently necessary, and an aluminium staff made up by connecting one-metre lengths is the most convenient type to use, as its length can easily be varied by adding or removing a section.

4. In the confines of a building, sightings are frequently very short so that the surveyor cannot see enough of the staff through the instrument to be sure of the reading. In this circumstance the surveyor directs the staffholder to move a pencil point up and down the staff until it is bisected by the cross-hairs. The surveyor or the staffholder can then take the reading direct from the staff.

Using a tape and rod only, heighting information can be booked either on a sketch section or on the sketch floor plan. Heights booked on a plan should be distinguished from linear measurements by placing them in a circle adjacent to the point where the height is taken. Normally, floor-to-ceiling, head and sill heights are booked on the sketch plan. Floor-to-floor heights and heights related to staircase and roof constructions are booked on the section.

The following should be measured in each room and internal space:

1. Floor-to-ceiling height. This is most conveniently measured at a door opening, with the door opened into the room. By placing the rod against the opening stile of the door and sliding it upwards until contact is made with the ceiling, the position of the bottom of the rod can be marked discretely on the stile with a pencil, and the remaining distance from the mark to the floor measured separately, and added to the length of the rod to give the total floor-to-ceiling height. This method ensures that the rod is held vertically and clears any projecting cornice that would prevent the measurement being made against a wall.

2. Sill and head heights of window and door openings (Figure 6.5). These should be taken as running dimensions using the floor as a datum. The floor-to-sill height is generally taken to the upper surface of any sill board in the case of windows. If the window does not have a sill board then the height is taken to the underside of timber sills or exposed stone surrounds. The floor-to-head height is taken to the soffit of the structural opening.

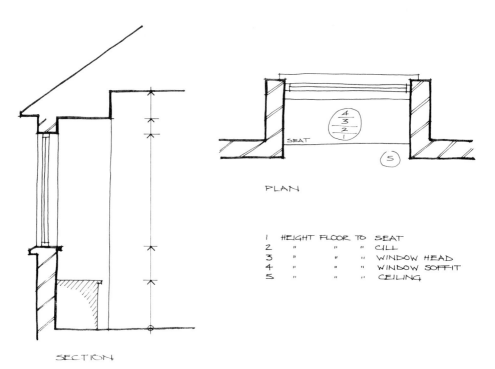

PLAN

1 HEIGHT FLOOR TO SEAT
2   "   "   " CILL
3   "   "   " WINDOW HEAD
4   "   "   " WINDOW SOFFIT
5   "   "   " CEILING

SECTION

Figure 6.5 Booking height dimension.

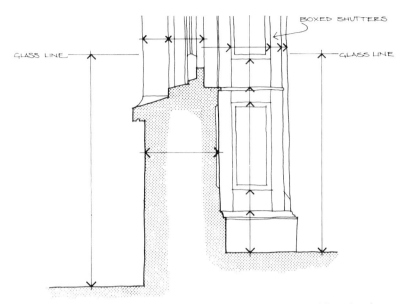

Figure 6.6 Glassline used to relate ground level to ground floor level.

3. More detailed sketches showing the dimensions of window seats, sills, bottom rails of sashes, position of the glass line, and other detail can be prepared, if required, related to the sill height as a datum (Figure 6.6).

Floor-to-floor heights can usually be established at staircase positions (Figure 6.7). If there is a well, it can easily be taped. On straight flights, with

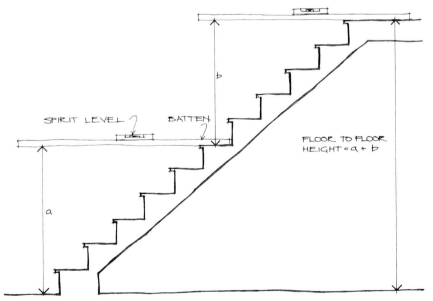

Figure 6.7 Measuring floor-to-floor heights at a staircase.

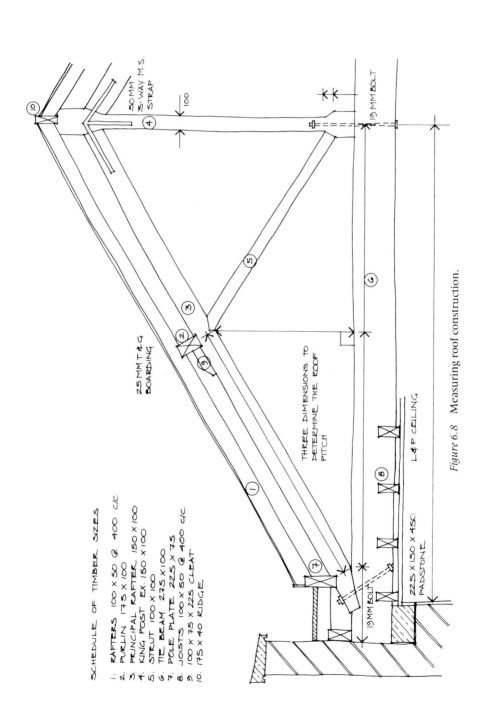

SCHEDULE OF TIMBER SIZES

1. RAFTERS 100 × 50 @ 400 c/c
2. PURLIN 175 × 100
3. PRINCIPAL RAFTER 150 × 100
4. KING POST EX. 150 × 100
5. STRUT 100 × 100
6. TIE BEAM 275 × 100
7. POLE PLATE 225 × 75
8. JOISTS 100 × 50 @ 400 c/c
9. 100 × 75 × 225 CLEAT
10. 175 × 40 RIDGE

25 MM T & G BOARDING

50 MM
3-WAY M.S. STRAP

100

19 MM BOLT

19 MM BOLT

THREE DIMENSIONS TO DETERMINE THE ROOF PITCH

L & P CEILING

225 × 150 × 450 PADSTONE

19 MM BOLT

Figure 6.8 Measuring roof construction.

no well, the dimension may have to be derived by taking more than one measurement.

The thickness of floors can be derived by subtracting the floor-to-ceiling height from the floor-to-floor height. However, it is prudent to measure the floor thickness at the stairwell if possible. The depth of floor joists can be deduced by subtracting appropriate thicknesses for floor boards and ceiling finishes from the total floor depth. The spacing of joists can be ascertained by measuring between rows of floor brads. The width of joists can only be determined by lifting a floor-board and exposing for measurement.

In roof voids most of the measurement is carried out using a pocket tape and a rod. If bats are present in a roof void, care must be exercised whilst measuring to avoid disturbing or damaging their roosts as they are a protected species under the Wildlife and Countryside Act, 1981. The following information should be booked:

1. The section sizes of all the members making up the roof construction and their centre-to-centre spacings (Figure 6.8).
2. The angle of pitch. This can be determined in two ways:
   ♦ Taking three measurements so that the pitch can be plotted by trilateration.
   ♦ By setting a folding rod so that one arm is parallel to the ceiling joists, the other parallel to the rafter line, and transferring the angle so formed to a sheet of paper by drawing along each arm of the rod (Figure 6.9).
3. The position and size of chimney flues and other walls built up into or through the roof void.

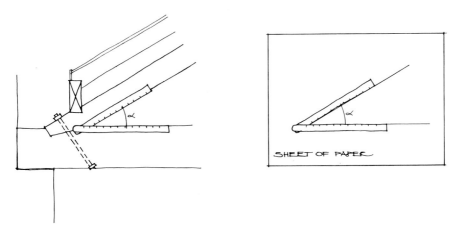

Figure 6.9 Using a folding rod to measure the angle of a pitched roof.

MEASURING EXTERNALLY

If the interior of the building has been measured as described above there will be little that is not already tied in. All that remains to be done will be to measure around the exterior of the building at ground floor level and to take such supplementary measurements as may be necessary to locate purely external features in relation to their internal counterparts.

At first sight, it may seem to be a pointless exercise to measure in the positions of door and window openings externally since their position can be derived from internal measurements and wall thicknesses. However, fully surveying the exterior at ground floor level provides an important independent check on the internal survey. If the survey is accurate, then on plotting out the positions of openings in the external walls, the positions will correspond, whichever set of dimensions is used. Misclosures must be investigated and remeasuring carried out if necessary.

In carrying out the survey around the building to pick up all the features at or about ground floor level, take sufficient dimensions to tie in projecting wings and re-entrant features (Figure 6.10). If columns are present, it is usual practice to locate them by running dimensions to their centre-lines and noting their diameters and base sizes (Figure 6.11).

When measuring the position of detail at high level on the elevations of the building, the following principles should be followed:

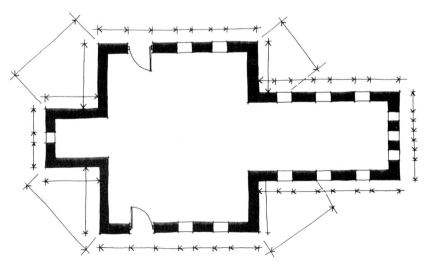

Figure 6.10 Tying in projecting wings and re-entrant features.

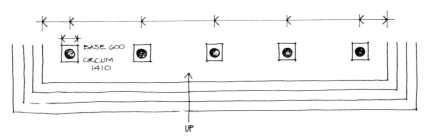

Figure 6.11 Measuring colonnades.

1. Establish a reliable horizontal datum to which vertical measurements may be related. Suitable features to act as a datum would be a plinth course, a string course or the eaves. The relationship of the selected datum to the ground floor (or other known horizontal feature) should be measured and noted, and likewise the relationship to any new datum that may be selected.
2. Vertical measurements up or down from the datum may be taken using either a tape or a rod (Figure 6.12). Where measurements are taken by leaning out from upper floor window openings, care should be taken to work safely.
3. If a high-level horizontal measurement cannot conveniently or safely be taken from a window opening, it may be possible, by reference to

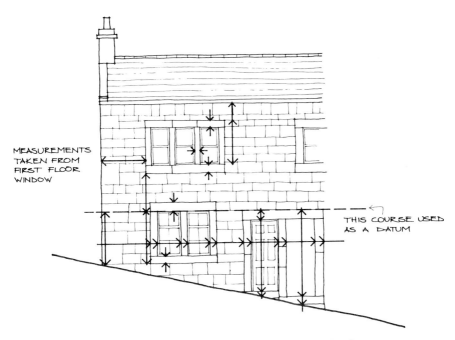

Figure 6.12 Measuring elevations by tape and rod.

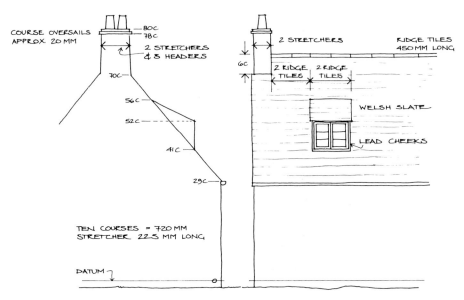

Figure 6.13 Measuring elevations by reference to brick courses and the lengths of ridge tiles.

perpend joints, to judge a position at a lower level vertically below, where a horizontal measurement can more readily be taken.

4. If direct measurements cannot be taken because a feature is not accessible, building products of a standard size may be used to make a reasonably accurate estimate, whether it be the length of ridge tiles, header and stretcher faces of brickwork, or regular course heights in masonry construction (Figure 6.12). The size of the feature used can be measured in a convenient position and this dimension used for calculation purposes. When measuring brick courses it is good practice to measure ten courses and divide the dimension by ten to establish the height of a single course: in this way any minor variation in mortar courses or bricks is averaged out.

5. Timber-framed buildings, where the structural framing is exposed, are measured following the principles outlined above. However, if the frame has become distorted or if the arrises of individual timbers are irregular, it may be necessary to fix a grid of nylon lines to the face of the building so that each line provides a reliable horizontal or vertical datum from which measurements may be taken (Figure 6.13). The lines are secured by nails driven into the joints between the timbers and the infill panels, taking care not to damage the building fabric, and each line checked with a spirit level before being relied upon. To avoid the horizontal lines sagging, nails should be at centres not more than two metres apart. The size of the grid will depend on the circumstances.

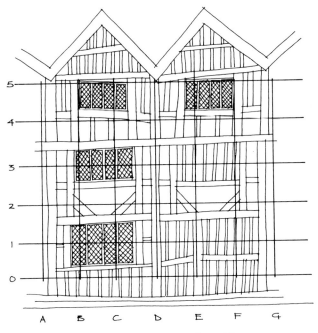

Figure 6.14   Using a string grid.

MEASURING DETAIL

Arches

Sufficient dimensions need to be taken to establish the centre(s) from which the curve(s) making up the arch are struck.

For a simple segmental arch, the span and rise at the crown must be recorded. When these are plotted out to a convenient scale, the arch can be constructed by drawing a line to connect the springing point to the crown, which is then bisected with a perpendicular line. The point where this perpendicular bisecting line cuts the centreline is the centre from which the arch is struck (Figure 6.15). The centres for Gothic arches can be found in a similar manner (Figure 6.16).

Appendix C shows the setting-out points for the most commonly met arch forms.

Entasis

Entasis, that is the swelling or curving outwards along the line of a column shaft, is intended to counteract the optical illusion which gives a tapering shaft bounded by straight lines the impression of curving upwards. It may be recorded by taping the circumference of the column at regular intervals

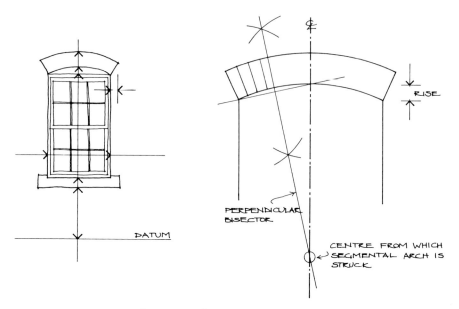

Figure 6.15 Plotting a segmental arch.

along its shaft, and booking both the circumference and the height at which it is measured (Figure 6.17). When plotting the column in elevation, the various diameters can be calculated using the formula:

$$\text{diameter} = \text{circumference}/\pi$$

Bar tracery

Patterns for bar tracery were designed and set out geometrically using compasses. In order to plot window tracery successfully, the centres from which the various curves making up the design were struck must be established by careful measurement, possibly using a string grid to establish the coordinates of cusps and similar features (Figures 6.18 and 6.19). The surveyor should carefully analyse the window to identify and then to measure in the skeleton outline of the design before moving on to record the detail.

Mouldings

The profiles of mouldings in timber and stone can be measured in a number of ways:

1. Using a '*Mimic*™ instant shape tracer', a device 150 × 80 mm in size comprising a metal frame in which 165 identical steel needles are held

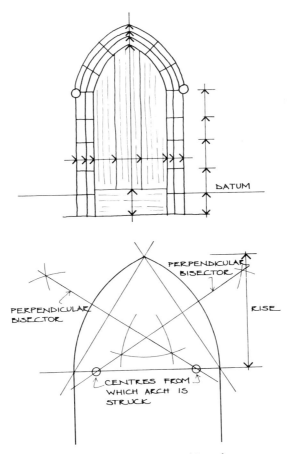

Figure 6.16   Plotting a Gothic arch.

by friction. The device is firmly pressed against the moulding to be measured and the needles take up an identical full-sized profile which can be traced onto paper with a pencil.

2. A strip of lead can be dressed around the moulding and then carefully removed, to record the profile by tracing around it.

3. If there is any open joint, say between adjacent stones, a piece of paper can be inserted into it and the profile traced directly on the paper.

4. Holding a straight edge, say a measuring rod, vertically against the moulding, offsets may be taken using a pocket tape. A vernier caliper can also be useful for intricate measurement.

Figure 6.20 illustrates these various techniques, and some common Classic and Gothic moulding profiles are given in Appendix D.

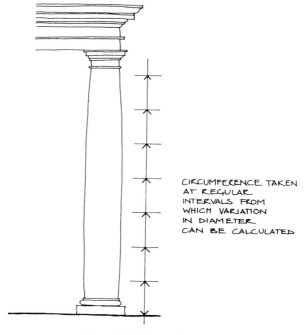

CIRCUMFERENCE TAKEN
AT REGULAR
INTERVALS FROM
WHICH VARIATION
IN DIAMETER
CAN BE CALCULATED

Figure 6.17 Measuring entasis.

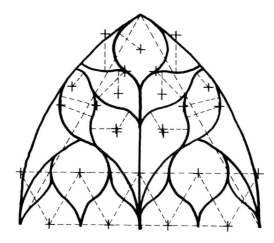

Figure 6.18 Analysis of the centres of the tracery at St Denys, Sleaford, Lincolnshire (after J. A. and R. Brandon).

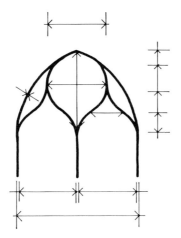

Figure 6.19 Measuring tracery.

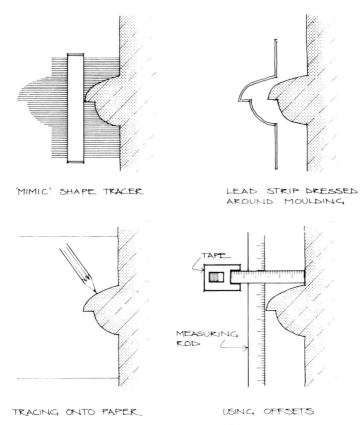

'MIMIC' SHAPE TRACER

LEAD STRIP DRESSED
AROUND MOULDING

TRACING ONTO PAPER

USING OFFSETS

Figure 6.20 Measuring mouldings.

CHAPTER SEVEN

Building Surveys III: Plotting and Presentation

PLOTTING THE SURVEY

The following equipment is required for plotting a measured building survey and producing the finished drawing:

Drawing-board
Tee square
Steel straight edge
Adjustable set square
Scale rule
Spring bow compasses
Beam compasses
Pencils and technical pens
Eraser and eraser shield
Stencils
Dry transfer material
Paper
Draughting tape

The survey is plotted initially onto cartridge paper or polyester draughting film (avoid plotting on tracing paper as it is not dimensionally stable, being affected by changes in temperature and humidity) following the general principles described for a chain survey in Chapter 3. However, the process is slightly more complex and the following procedures are recommended:

Table 7.1 Recommended plotting scales

Site and key plans	1 : 500
Plans, sections and elevations for whole buildings:	
Small buildings of a domestic scale	1 : 50
Medium-sized buildings, e.g. churches	1 : 100
Large buildings, e.g. warehouses/factories	1 : 200
Detailed plans, sections and elevations of parts of buildings	
The more detail that is required to be shown, the larger the scale should be, for example:	
Panelling, chancel screens, window tracery	$\begin{cases} 1 : 20 \\ 1 : 10 \end{cases}$
Ornament, mouldings	$\begin{cases} 1 : 5 \\ 1 : 1 \end{cases}$

1. Decide on a suitable scale(s): those listed in Table 7.1 are recommended.
2. Starting with the ground floor plan, take the longest straight wall and plot to the chosen scale its length and thickness, allowing for any variations in thickness, and mark the positions at which any internal walls make a junction with it. With this wall as a baseline, plot in outline the various rooms and spaces in the building by constructing triangles from the wall lengths and diagonals recorded on the booking sheets. Use the longest lines and diagonals first, before working down to the shorter lengths, until the skeleton outline of the plan is completely developed. At each stage, as the plotting progresses, use check and overall dimensions to discover any errors or inaccuracies. If discrepancies are found, corrective action should be taken before proceeding since errors can quickly build up.
3. Once the ground floor plan has been plotted in outline and considered to be correct, the positions and details of door and window openings, staircases and other features can be added.

   Apply checks on the accuracy of the plotting by matching measurements of both sides of the wall at openings.

   When drawing staircases, once the top and bottom risers of flights have been plotted, the positions of individual steps are best located by dividing the space between geometrically. For example, if there are eight risers to be shown in a flight, using any convenient scale, lay a scale rule obliquely between the top and bottom riser positions so that the number of graduations on the scale is an exact multiple of seven (as the number of treads in a flight will always be one less than the number of risers), and mark off each riser position against the appropriate gradation (Figure 7.1).
4. From the final plot of the ground floor plan, copy a skeleton plan of the

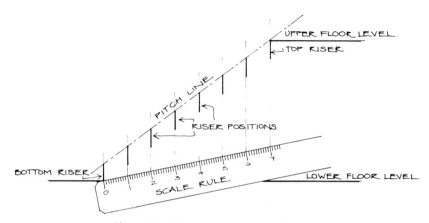

Figure 7.1 Plotting the positions of risers.

main lines of the construction which can then be used to form the basis of the first-floor plans. If polyester film is used, trace the ground floor arrangement directly onto it. If cartridge paper is used, 'prick' through the corners of the building onto a fresh piece of cartridge paper using a steel pricker made from a spare compass point. The pricker marks are then joined up in pencil to form the base plan on which to plot the first-floor plan.

In plotting upper floor plans, be vigilant for structural walls reducing in thickness with height, and check the accuracy of the plotting at every opportunity.

5. Proceed to plot the remaining upper floors, basement and roof plans along the lines described above.

6. Sections and elevations are conveniently plotted alongside one another using the dimensions from the booking sheets, and the normal draughting practice of projecting already scaled dimensions between plans, sections or elevations by means of a tee square and set square.

When drawing a staircase in section, once the position of top and the bottom of the flight have been plotted, use the principle of geometrical division described in (3) to determine the position of individual treads and risers, and thus the profile of the flight (Figure 7.2).

7. If the survey and the plotting have been properly executed, there should be no discrepancy between any of the drawings produced.

PREPARING THE FINAL SURVEY DRAWING

The final survey drawing is produced by tracing off the plots on to tracing paper or polyester film in ink and/or pencil, as preferred.

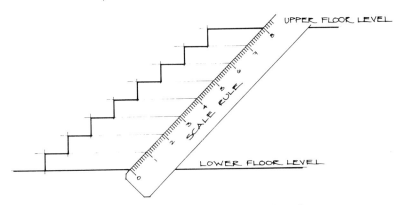

Figure 7.2 Plotting the positions of treads.

Layout of the drawings

Wherever possible, arrange the plans, sections and elevations on a single sheet following the principles set out below:

1. Place the plan of the lowest floor at the bottom left of the sheet. Plans for single, secular buildings should have the wall of the principal elevation facing towards the bottom of the sheet, churches should be orientated conventionally. Plans of building complexes should place grid north at the top of the sheet.
2. Successive floor plans are drawn alongside the lowest floor plan in their correct sequence and in the same orientation.
3. Place the front elevation immediately above the ground floor plan and the other elevations in a row and lined up with the front elevation.
4. The section(s) and site plan (if any) are placed where they will conveniently fit on the sheet and give it a balanced appearance.
5. The inter-relationship of plans, sections and elevations should be recognized by placing them on the drawing in such a way that common features are in either horizontal or vertical alignment as appropriate.

Figure 7.3 shows a typical drawing layout.

Inevitably, it will not always be possible to lay out the whole survey on one sheet. In cases where this arises the guiding rule for sheet arrangement should be logical presentation: all plans on one drawing, say, and sections on another.

Annotation

Graphical representations alone will not convey all the relevant information to the reader, and must be supplemented by annotations to the drawing. In annotating drawings the following principles should be observed:

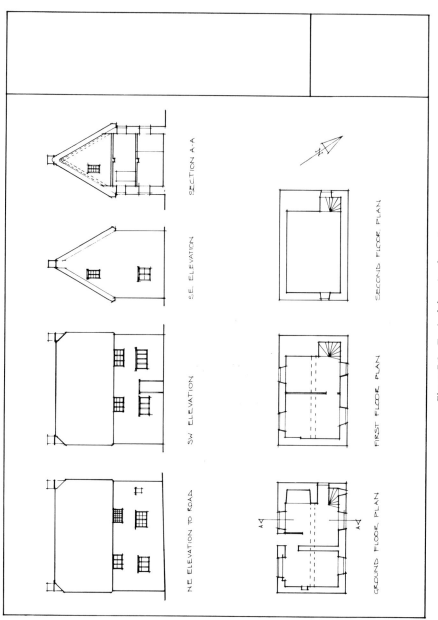

NE ELEVATION TO ROAD

SW ELEVATION

S.E. ELEVATION

SECTION A-A

GROUND FLOOR PLAN

FIRST FLOOR PLAN

SECOND FLOOR PLAN

Figure 7.3 Typical drawing layout.

1. The size of lettering should be appropriate to its function. In diminishing order of size/boldness should be:

   Main titles, e.g. Survey of the Castle of Otranto
   Drawing labels, e.g. Section A–A
   Names identifying spaces, e.g. Machine Shop No. 2
   Grouped notes on construction, materials and finishes

2. Lines of lettering should be placed parallel to the bottom of the drawing, with all characters of uniform size and evenly spaced.
3. Drawing labels should either be centred below a drawing or aligned with the extreme left-hand side of the drawing being captioned.
4. The sections should be the main foci for information about materials, finishes and construction. The information should be marshalled into convenient blocks, each dealing with a particular element of construction and placed on the drawing adjacent to the item described. The information in each block should follow a logical sequence describing each layer of construction as it is encountered, starting a new line for each component. For example:

   Random Swithland slates
   Battens
   25 mm t & g boarding
   100×50 mm s.w. rafters @ 450 c/c
   20 mm lath and plaster ceiling

Roof member sizes can be conveniently scheduled:

   Queen post trusses @ 1800 mm c/c
   Principal rafter 175×150 mm
   Tie beam 300×150 mm
   Queen posts ex 175×150 mm
   Straining beam 175×150 mm
   Straining sill 150×50 mm
   Struts 100×100 mm
   Cleats $150 \times 75 \times 225$ mm
   Purlins 175×100 mm
   Common rafters 100×50 mm
   Ridge 175×30 mm

Lettering can be carried out freehand (using fine pencil guidelines to control the height of the characters), by means of stencils or dry transfer lettering, or a combination of methods. Many surveyors use stencil or dry transfer lettering for main titles and labels, and freehand lettering for grouped notes.

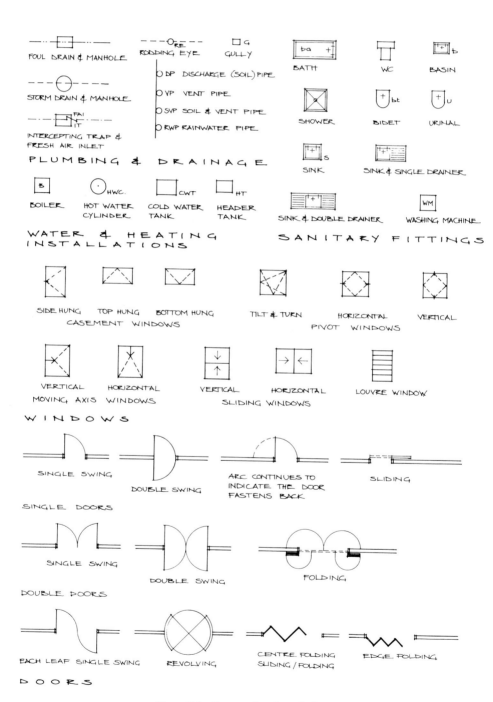

Figure 7.4 Conventional symbols.

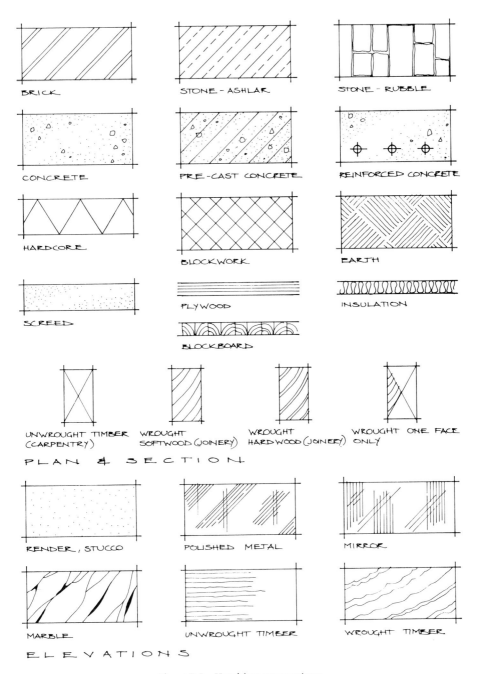

BRICK

STONE - ASHLAR

STONE - RUBBLE

CONCRETE

PRE-CAST CONCRETE

REINFORCED CONCRETE

HARDCORE

BLOCKWORK

EARTH

SCREED

PLYWOOD

INSULATION

BLOCKBOARD

UNWROUGHT TIMBER (CARPENTRY)

WROUGHT SOFTWOOD (JOINERY)

WROUGHT HARDWOOD (JOINERY)

WROUGHT ONE FACE ONLY

PLAN & SECTION

RENDER, STUCCO

POLISHED METAL

MIRROR

MARBLE

UNWROUGHT TIMBER

WROUGHT TIMBER

ELEVATIONS

Figure 7.5 Hatching conventions.

PRESENTATION

In preparing the final drawings normal architectural drawing conventions should be followed. British Standard 1192, *Construction Drawing Practice* Parts 1, 2 and 3, and the Royal Commission on the Historical Monuments of England's *Recording Historic Buildings: A Descriptive Specification* both contain useful advice. The main points to note are:

1. Vary line thicknesses to give the drawing 'life' and make it easier to 'read'. For most work a minimum of two technical pens is recommended: one with a nib to give a line thickness of 0.5 mm and the other 0.25 mm. The thicker pen should be used to denote load-bearing walls, where they are cut by horizontal or vertical section lines, the outline of elevations and ground lines; the thinner one can be used for details such as doors, windows and staircases, and for lines beyond the cutting plane of section lines and hatching.
2. Use conventional symbols for showing windows, doors, sanitary fittings and so forth (Figure 7.4).
3. Denote materials using standard conventional hatchings (Figure 7.5).
4. The completed survey drawing(s) should contain the following information:
   - Notes on the sizes of structural members, materials and finishes.
   - Floor levels, changes in level, and ceiling heights dimensioned on the sections.
   - The direction of stair rises on plan, with each riser numbered.
   - The positions of service entry points, plant and machinery, sanitary fittings, below-ground drainage, soil and vent stacks, rainwater pipes.
   - Lines to indicate the positions where sections have been taken on plan and the direction of view.
   - A north point.
   - Labelling of drawings, such as Section A–A.
   - A scale bar in metric and Imperial.
   - Border and a title panel. The title panel should contain the following information: description of the sheet content, the scale as a representative fraction, the date, name(s) of the surveyor(s), job/drawing reference number.
5. It may be intended to colour the prints from the survey using a water colour wash or felt-tip pen. The conventional colours for common building materials are given in Table 7.2.

Table 7.2   Conventional colours for representing
building materials

Brick	Vermilion
Cast iron	Payne's grey
Cast or reconstructed stone	Viridian
Concrete	Hooker's green
Earth	Sepia
Faience, tiles	Chrome orange
Glass	Pale blue wash
Planed and moulded timber	Burnt sienna
Plaster	Terra verde
Sawn timber	Raw sienna
Steel	Purple
Stone	Cobalt blue
Wrought iron	Prussian blue

ARCHIVING

Consideration should be given to depositing copies of completed surveys of buildings of architectural or historic interest in a public archive for safekeeping, and to make the information accessible to researchers and others having an interest in the building.

For buildings of national importance, the body to contact is the Royal Commission responsible for maintaining the National Buildings Record in its area. These are:

England: Royal Commission on the Historic Monuments of England, Fortress House, 23 Savile Row, London W1X 1AB

Scotland: Royal Commission on the Historic and Ancient Monuments of Scotland, 54 Melville Street, Edinburgh, EH3 7HF

Wales: Royal Commission on the Historic and Ancient Monuments of Wales, Crown Building, Plas Cruig, Aberystwyth, Dyfed SY23 2HP

Locally, consider depositing copies with the County Record Office and with the local authority for inclusion in its Site and Monuments Record.

ANALYTICAL AND CONDITION SURVEYS

Once a basic measured survey has been completed, prints from it provide a useful medium on which to record additional survey information, for example:

1. Evidence to help give a better understanding of how the building has been altered and adapted over the years could be noted on the drawing in the appropriate positions. Such evidence would include:
   - Differences in material, construction technique, and architectural style and decoration.
   - Structural independence of adjoining parts of the building.
   - Blocked door and window openings.
   - Inserted openings in walls.

2. Disrepair and its extent could be noted as a preliminary to preparing specifications or schedules of work.

CHAPTER EIGHT

Architectural Photography and Related Surveying Techniques

INTRODUCTION

Techniques for measuring and recording built fabric can be described as either direct or indirect in their application, depending on the methods and equipment employed.

In many surveys it is possible to measure physically the subject matter using traditional means, and to plot manually the measurements to form a two-dimensional scale record of acceptable accuracy. There are times, however, when it is neither practical nor safe to take such measurements, including cases where buildings are in an unstable condition or fabric lies out of reach of ladders and telescopic rods. Consideration must then be given to obtaining the required data by other means.

Indirect or remote measurement and recording can take a number of forms, based either on the use of electronic and optical surveying equipment, as described previously, or on photography and other imaging techniques.

RECORDING BY PHOTOGRAPHY

A photograph provides a record of an event or object at a particular moment in time, and contains many categories or layers of information that would otherwise require detailed written description or sketching in order to capture. Whilst both these have been used to good effect, they can suffer from subjectivity and are open to interpretation. A photograph, on the other hand, can provide an objective record that offers a source of latent information for instant consumption or later examination. This is particularly the case when concerned with building conservation (Noble, 1982).

Early experiments with optical equipment, and later photographic processes, used this ability to communicate information in many ways, and much of the pioneering work of the nineteenth century made use of buildings and architecture, as well as landscape and nature.

PHOTOGRAPHY AND PHOTOGRAPHIC EQUIPMENT

The purpose of record photography is to convey as much information as is required for a particular purpose in a simple and direct manner, without being obscured or distorted by expressions of artistry.

In order to achieve satisfactory results it is important that equipment is selected wisely and its practical applications and limitations are understood. Most handbooks on photography provide useful introductions and give references to more advanced texts, with those of particular merit noted below. With regard to the particular problems of photographing historic buildings and their interiors, the reader is referred to Terry Buchanan's excellent book *Photographing Historic Buildings for the Record* (1983).

Specialized architectural photography requires specific equipment, such as a monorail view camera of typically 4 × 5 in. (10.2 × 12.7 cm) or 10 × 8 in. (20. 3 × 17.8 cm) format that allows swings, tilts and shifts, or 'camera movements', of the lens position to be made relative to the film plane. This chapter, however, concentrates on the use of the lighter, more mobile and readily understood 35 mm single lens reflex camera system as a tool for recording built fabric, based on a camera body, interchangeable lenses and relevant accessories.

Cameras

The single lens reflex (SLR) camera allows through-the-lens viewing, which avoids parallax errors caused by displacement between the views of the lens and direct vision viewfinder when moving closer to the subject. This is a particular problem of 35 mm compact cameras that require a correction to be borne in mind when viewing the subject.

Almost all SLR cameras have through-the-lens (TTL) light metering, which means that external or hand-held exposure meters are not always required. This metering may be manual, which requires the user to set both aperture and shutter speed, or automatic, giving a choice of shutter or aperture priority systems. Automatic metering is useful for architectural photography as it instantly adjusts for changing light conditions.

Multi-mode cameras offer a choice of either aperture priority or shutter priority, and many automatic cameras have a manual override facility.

Lenses

The quality of a camera lens is reflected in its price, and cost-cutting here will have consequences for the quality of the photography produced. Whilst it is often stated that the best lens for a camera is that designed specifically for it, it is nevertheless possible to obtain good quality lenses from various manufacturers. It is wise to shop around when purchasing lenses, whether new or second-hand, and to be prepared to try the lenses in the showroom until satisfied with the feel of the action, weight and general balance of the lens on your own camera body.

The choice of lens depends greatly on what is expected of it, and opting for a good range of reasonably priced lenses is recommended. The most useful lenses for architectural recording will be those of wide angle (say 28–50 mm) and mid-range telephoto (say 50–150 mm) focal lengths allowing full coverage and the opportunity for some detail work.

The automatic control of exposures as noted above typically requires the user to select either the shutter speed suitable for the subject, or the lens aperture. Whilst the former is ideal for action photography where action is frozen, architectural work benefits from the control over depth of field offered by selecting the aperture, despite having to consider the effect on shutter speed and hence the risk of camera shake in low-light conditions.

Aperture selection controls the amount of light reaching the film such that the dimmer the conditions, the larger the aperture size or 'stop' necessary to achieve a constant light level. The manner in which the aperture is selected is based on *f numbers*, mathematical factors calculated by dividing the focal length by the diameter of the aperture: the smaller the *f* number, the larger the aperture. Each *f* number lets in twice as much light as the number on one side of it and half as much as the number on the other side.

The size of the aperture also affects the definition of the image, so that at maximum aperture the sharpness is greater at the centre than at the corners. Stopping down the lens improves this corner definition, and also that at the centre of the image.

Depth of field is affected by changing the *f* number, so that a decrease in aperture size will increase the depth of field and extend the distance between the nearest and furthest points of the subject that are acceptably sharp.

In considering the selection of photographic lenses it is worth noting their particular influences on the subject matter recorded. Standard or normal lenses for 35 mm cameras have focal lengths of between 40 and 58 mm, usually 50 mm, the precise figure of 43.3 mm being related to the diagonal measurement of the film format. Such a standard lens 'sees' the same angle of view as our own eyes, or more correctly, one eye.

A wide-angle lens, having a focal length less than 50 mm, includes a wider field of view, increases the sense of depth (particularly in nearby objects), and reduces the relative size of elements in the picture; whereas a telephoto lens, with a focal length greater than 50 mm, takes in a narrower field, foreshortens the perception of depth, and enlarges the relative size of distant objects. In essence, the depth of field shortens as the focal length increases given a constant f number.

The shift in apparent perspective noticed in wide-angle photography, known as the 'wide-angle effect', causes objects near the camera to appear disproportionately large and distant objects to be reduced in size and look comparatively flat. Objects close to the edges and corners of the frame tend also to become elongated. Telephoto lenses pull in distant objects, making them appear larger, but reduce the depth of field. As depth of field is thus affected, so focusing and shutter speeds are critical, particularly when the camera is hand-held. As a rule of thumb, choose a shutter speed whose reciprocal is as large as the focal length of the lens, for example $1/125$ s with a 100 mm lens and $1/500$ s with a 500 mm lens.

One of the main problems encountered in photographing buildings is the presence of converging vertical lines, sometimes known as 'keystoning'. These are allowed for in real life by the brain creating a mental image based on the previous knowledge that the building does not taper. Photography, however, records these effects of perspective, requiring specific correction to be considered:

1. Increase the height of the camera so that it is located ideally at the mid-height of the subject.
2. Use a wide-angle lens to photograph the building from a distance, enlarge, and then crop the unwanted foreground during or after printing.
3. Make use of specialized equipment such as perspective-control or 'shift' lenses for 35 mm cameras, or larger-format monorail view cameras.
4. Make corrections at the printing stage by tilting the baseboard and/or negative carrier.

Shift lenses are constructed to allow their glass elements to be physically moved from their normal positions in an attempt to replicate in a limited way the camera movements of a view camera (Figure 8.1). These lenses are

Figure 8.1   Perspective-control lens.

made by only a small number of manufacturers to fit their own cameras, are relatively expensive and have wide-angle characteristics, typically 28 mm or 35 mm. One particular manufacturer does produce a shift lens that is also capable of tilting.

Whilst shift lenses are particularly useful for architectural photography, they also allow obstructions to be avoided by shifting the lens relative to the obstruction. They can also be used to produce extended images by shifting the lens from one side to the other, enabling a montage to be formed of the resulting prints.

Accessories

Photographic accessories are a topic in their own right, but for architectural recording they can be limited to those items that have been found to be of practical use on site.

Camera supports

Tripods and other forms of support allow a camera to remain steady during a lengthy exposure required by poor light conditions or when stopping down the lens to increase the depth of field, so avoiding blurred images. Whilst many models are lightweight and highly portable, it is better to choose a weighty version so that it remains stable even in windy conditions. Additional weight can be provided by hanging an equipment bag from the central column in certain situations.

The degree of flexibility and manoeuvrability required from a tripod is a matter of choice, but a heavy-duty model such as the Bembo Mk. 2 manufactured by Kennet Engineering can be used in all conditions. An adjustable head with either a ball and socket or tilt-pan arrangement with control arm gives complete flexibility, the Manfrotto Standard 029 three-way tilt-pan head complete with two built-in level bubbles being found to give excellent service. These two items of equipment are shown in Figure 8.2.

High-level photography for recording purposes, or inspection of inaccessible parts of a building, can be undertaken using such facilities as

Figure 8.2 Tripod and adjustable head.

extending hoists or platforms used for street-lamp cleaning and other operations. Photography in windy conditions at such heights can make the choice of a fast shutter speed essential.

Alternatively, a number of firms provide a specialized service using hydraulic or mechanical masts that can be fitted with either a still or video camera giving coverage of high-level fabric. Smaller masts can be used for recording the inside faces of walls, such as found with standing architectural remains, providing visual information for assessing condition and scheduling works of repair or consolidation. Limited use may also be made of radio-controlled aeroplanes or helicopters, kites and tethered balloons for acquiring high-level coverage. Figure 8.3 shows a telescopic mast on top of which is mounted a remotely operated camera.

In conjunction with the use of a tripod, the shutter should be activated indirectly to avoid camera movement, either by a cable release that may be mechanical, pneumatic or electronic, or a delayed-action self-timer mechanism if provided.

Figure 8.3   High-level photographic recording.

Films

The use of a stable tripod or support means that a slow film speed can be employed to achieve clarity of detail and a grain-free image, and slow shutter speeds can be operated in low light conditions without the risk of camera shake. It should be noted, however, that in normal photochemical reactions, the formation of a developed emulsion is directly proportional to the total exposure, measured as a product of intensity and time such that $H = Et$, where H is the chemical product, E the illuminance (lux = lx) and t the exposure time (lux seconds = lxs). This reciprocity exists only over a limited range of intensities and times for the exposure. At very high intensities (very long exposures) and very low intensities (very short exposures) the photographical process works much less efficiently than at intermediate exposures. In practice, very short exposures do not present a problem for the recording of built fabric, but very long exposures require extended exposure times. In this case it is wise to 'bracket' a series of different exposures up and down from the nominally correct setting in order to increase the chance of a successful result. The effects of 'reciprocity failure' are less serious with black-and-white film than with colour.

The choice of film itself requires careful consideration, as selection is very much based on what is required from the photography. It is generally accepted that black-and-white photography, when processed to a specific standard, is preferred for architectural recording. This is especially so if the results are to be used in an archive where storage and retrieval are being considered because the long-term stability of colour images has not yet been sufficiently proven.

Whatever the purpose of the photography in the first instance, it is suggested that both black-and-white and colour be used to record the subject concerned as each can satisfy different requirements. Often, colour slides or projection transparencies are used for lecture purposes, whilst black-and-white prints provide an accessible form of archive source. In this respect, transparencies have a greater permanence than negatives, pro-vided they are not used for projection. Whatever the final decision, it is fundamental in establishing a useful collection to store and index negatives and slides in a safe and organized manner.

A photographic image is obtained through the use of recorded patterns of radiated electromagnetic light. Electromagnetic radiation is a form of radiant energy, being subdivided into various categories of which visible light is the name given to that part of the spectrum to which the human eye is sensitive. The other wavebands, radio waves, microwaves, infra-red, ultra-violet, X-ray, gamma ray and cosmic ray photons, have either greater or shorter wavelengths than visible light.

In considering most general black-and-white photography, an image is formed when light rays reflected from the subject strike the light-sensitive emulsion of the film and cause the silver halides to break down and form black metallic silver grains. It is the concentration of these grains that determines the highlights, mid-tones and shadows, or 'density', of the visible image during processing.

The projection of the rays of light onto the film or image plane is controlled by the lens, and this may lead to a displacement of these rays that foreshortens the projected image and thus removes the three-dimensional quality of depth from the resulting photograph. This projection through a single point is known as a 'central projection' and will have implications for the use of such an image for indirect measurement as may be seen later.

Most black-and-white film used for general photography is classed as 'panchromatic', meaning that it possesses an emulsion that is sensitive to all the colours of the visible spectrum, and to a certain amount of ultra-violet light. This records light as tones of grey, with approximately the same relative brightness as appears to the observer. The resulting range of tones or densities representing the light and shade of the subject matter means that evaluation is more subjective than with colour photography.

Colour film is made up of a number of emulsions, one on top of the other, so that each responds to different parts of the visible spectrum. These multi-layer emulsion coatings can therefore achieve a full colour image with one exposure. It is necessary, however, to balance the film used with the intended light source, requiring either a daylight or tungsten film. Colour 35 mm negative film is made only for daylight use, whereas transparency films may be used in other conditions. Specialized film emulsions are available that are sensitive to certain parts of the electro-magnetic spectrum. These are covered in a number of standard texts.

The speed or rating of a film is specified under various standards in order to relate the light sensitivity of one film to another. The current international standard, ISO, shows a doubling of speed by a doubling of the number, this also being the basis for the American Standards system, ASA. For general black-and-white recording, Ilford FP4 medium-speed film, rated at ISO 125/22°, has been found to give good results.

Filters

Although black-and-white film is sensitive to all colours, correction or accentuation is often required in order to provide a realistic image or one with emphasis placed on a particular material. Filters are effective because they change the quality of light reaching the film, so that a colour filter will lighten the reproduction of objects its own colour, and darken those of complementary colours.

In practice, therefore, a yellow filter will darken a blue sky and lighten yellow stonework, green will darken red brickwork and lighten green foliage, orange will darken blue skies and lighten red brickwork, and red will darken blues and greens and lighten brickwork.

Specialized filters are also available: neutral-density filters reduce the light reaching the film without affecting either colour or contrast, and so, in effect, down-rate the film speed; polarizing filters absorb rays of light vibrating in certain directions and so avoid unwanted reflections; ultra-violet filters can be left attached to lenses all the time both to protect the lens and to reduce the effects of atmospheric haze; and skylight filters at varying densities reduce haze and excessive bluishness.

Flash

The basic artificial light source used in photography is produced by passing electricity through a tungsten wire, rather than by a fluorescent lamp. An electronic flash unit or manual flashgun produces a brief, but very bright, illumination that can either replace or enhance natural light levels, with results depending on the direction and quality of the light produced.

When the flash unit is mounted on the camera the resulting image is often harsh and flat, thus reducing the three-dimensional qualities of the subject. By moving the flash away from the camera this flat appearance is eliminated and shadows enhance the image. Alternatively, direct light from an on-camera source can be bounced off a suitable light-coloured surface to give a softer illumination, or it can be reduced by a diffuser.

An electronic flash unit should be synchronized to fire when the shutter is open by choosing the shutter speed appropriate for the flash model being used. Calculation of the correct aperture for the exposure is based on the flash-to-subject distance, and this is carried out automatically or manually.

Use of off-camera flash lighting using a synchronization lead can be increased with further flash sources fired simultaneously by slave units that react to the light energy given off by the main camera-connected flash.

Apart from limited fill-in lighting, the artificial illumination of large interiors cannot satisfactorily be achieved with simple flash units. Long timed exposures, which may be subject to 'reciprocity failure', can be used, but otherwise professional equipment and techniques will have to be considered. Further advice on this and techniques for lighting interior features generally can be found in Buchanan (1983).

Additional items

A number of small accessories have been found to be useful in recording built fabric:

1. In order to ensure horizontal and vertical alignment of the subject in the composition, a matt-finished gridded focusing screen can be fitted inside certain makes of camera.

2. A small spirit level is useful to ensure that the film plane is vertical.

3. A small plumb-bob, with white or brightly coloured line, can be used to provide a definite break on a façade when taking a series of photographs to be viewed as a continuous record.

4. Small boards, which will accept chinagraph or some other visible mark, or even a selection of cloakroom numbers, will allow photographs to be referenced back to written notes including location, date and other information.

5. Viewing a subject in a confined space from above or to the sides of the camera can be assisted with an additional viewfinder fitted to the rearsight, a number of which have full dioptic correction and can magnify part of the image for exact focusing.

ARCHITECTURAL PHOTOGRAPHY

The term 'architectural photography' describes the recording of buildings, monuments and other structures to provide a pure record, an illustration or a picture. In a practical sense this can take the form of a creative art, a mode of communication, a vehicle for nostalgia or a tool for other disciplines.

In using photography as a tool for the recording of built fabric it is important to consider the processes that are involved, as many can introduce distortions requiring modification or interpretation. Indeed, the claim that the camera never lies is often made without acknowledging the selectivity of its use and ignorance of the fourth dimension of time.

One of the most obvious ways in which a building can be readily photographed is to set up the camera directly in front of each wall, so that the plane of the subject wall and the film or image plane are parallel. The resulting square-on image can then provide a reasonably accurate record of the single plane of the wall to a scale defined by standard lens formulae.

The use of a central projection for such recording, however, suffers from four major drawbacks (Figure 8.4), as noted by Dallas (1980c, p. 396):

1. Displacement of the image caused by depth changes within the subject wall.

2. Changes of scale due to different depths within the wall.

3. Variations of scale across the photograph caused by a lack of parallelism

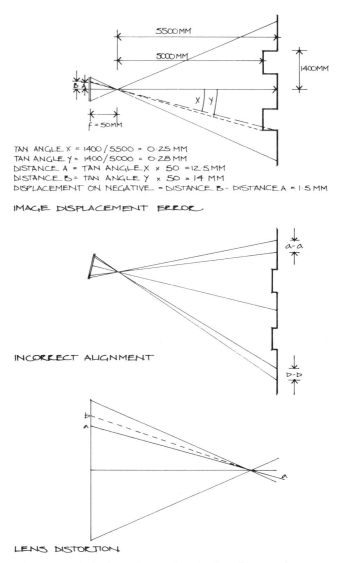

TAN ANGLE X = 1400 / 5500 = 0.25 MM
TAN ANGLE Y = 1400 / 5000 = 0.28 MM
DISTANCE A = TAN ANGLE X × 50 = 12.5 MM
DISTANCE B = TAN ANGLE Y × 50 = 14 MM
DISPLACEMENT ON NEGATIVE = DISTANCE B - DISTANCE A = 1.5 MM

IMAGE DISPLACEMENT ERROR

INCORRECT ALIGNMENT

LENS DISTORTION

Figure 8.4 Limitations of central-projection photography.

between the image plane and plane of the wall.
4. Inaccuracies caused when the light rays are distorted by the camera or enlarger.

In practice, the faces or façades of most buildings are not simple, single flat planes, but are instead made up of a number of different planes lying either in front of or behind the principal plane of the wall. These may be formed, for example, by a projecting porch or buttress, or a recessed window or chimney stack.

If a photograph were taken of such a building from directly in front of this wall, then the porch and buttress would be larger in scale, and the window and stack smaller than that of the principal plane on the resulting image, and their positions displaced. Were the camera to be wrongly set up, and the lens of poor optical quality, then further distortions would arise.

It is as a result of these limitations that simple photography as a means of providing architectural records of known dimensional accuracy is further extended by the use of revised procedures and equipment, including rectified photography and photogrammetry.

RECTIFIED PHOTOGRAPHY

In rectified photography, also termed photomontage, photo-mosaic or photo-drawing, the manner in which the image is recorded takes account of the limitations imposed by the central projection, and allows photographs of accuracies acceptable for architectural, and often archaeological, recording to be achieved without recourse to specialized equipment.

The process of photographic rectification is one that allows correction of image displacements caused by the effects of perspective, and, as such, originated from aerial survey where distortions caused by camera tilt could be eliminated by re-projection through a rectifying enlarger.

In its true sense, therefore, rectified photography corrects displacements, although the term is more often used with architectural recording for refining photographic procedures in order to produce square-on photographs of an acceptable dimensional accuracy to a known scale.

True rectification is, nevertheless, possible by angling the baseboard during printing, but this is governed by the Scheimflüg principle that requires the negative, lens plane and baseboard to intersect at the same point for the image to be in focus, and as such is a skilled operation requiring professional equipment.

The most important aspect of this form of indirect recording is the correct alignment of the camera so that the subject and image planes are parallel in both axes. This is best achieved by levelling the camera on a tripod so that the film plane is vertical, and then rotating the camera until it is parallel with the wall in question. Many of the better-quality tripod heads have built-in levelling bubbles; alternatively, a small spirit level may be held against the back of the camera body.

In order to ensure that the two planes are parallel it is easy and convenient to fit a gridded screen within the body of the camera, rotating the body until the lines of the screen line up with regular horizontal lines on the façade, such as the eaves or a string course. If the camera cannot be fitted with such a screen, then use the edges of the viewfinder in a similar manner.

There are other and more complicated ways in which this parallelism can be achieved, including the use of survey targets secured to the wall, and establishing the centreline of the wall using optical squares or constructed 3-4-5 triangles over which the tripod may be set up (Dallas, 1980c, p. 397).

The scale of the resulting image taken square-on or 'normal' to the façade can be calculated by the equation $S = f/h$, where S is the scale of the image, f is the focal length of the camera lens in millimetres, and h is the distance between image and subject planes in millimetres.

The most convenient way in which such images can be printed to scale is to record simple control dimensions of the façade using tape and rod, and enlarge the image on the baseboard during printing so that these dimensions relate to an acceptable scale by using a scale rule.

Although every factor within the procedure described can introduce its own variables, by using quality equipment a relatively high order of dimensional accuracy can be obtained on a façade with little or no depth variation. Figure 8.5 shows a suitable subject for rectified photography. Dallas (1980c, p. 398) considers an accuracy of ±40 mm at a scale of 1 : 50 to be possible.

Figure 8.5   Suitable subject for rectified photography.

Where the façade includes planes that are obviously recessed or projected forward, then these planes will be at a scale different from that of the principal plane. It is possible to photograph each plane, obtain separate dimensional control and print each to the required scale, these then being montaged together to produce a complete elevational photograph to a constant scale.

The presentation of rectified photographs, and more particularly montaged records, need not be by photographic print. Screening processes can be employed to provide film negatives for conventional dyeline printing, this allowing large-scale tonal images of elevations to be marked up and annotated as necessary for the work being undertaken.

PHOTOGRAMMETRY

Photogrammetry, in its widest sense, can be taken to mean the 'art, science, and technology of obtaining reliable information about physical objects and the environment through processes of recording, measuring, and interpreting photographic images and patterns of recorded radiant electromagnetic energy and other phenomena' (American Society of Photogrammetry).

In essence, therefore, photogrammetry makes use of photography for dimensional analysis, taking indirect measurements from the photographic image, rather than directly from the actual object.

The optical principles of photogrammetry are based largely on those that control our own sense of vision and depth perception: in essence, two views of the same object fused to give a mental image complete with three-dimensional perspective and depth. Continuing this analogy, the process of photogrammetry as a means of recording has been claimed to achieve with the camera all that is attainable unconsciously with the eyes, nervous system and brain (Harwood, 1982, p. 72).

As with photography in general, much of the pioneering work in photogrammetry was undertaken using architecture as the subject matter. The work of Albrecht Meydenbauer (1834–1921) in recording the architectural and historical monuments of Germany has since come to be recognized as the first systematic photogrammetric recording of architecture, popularizing the developing technique and forming the basis for much post-war reconstruction.

Whilst much has been written concerning the technicalities of this method for recording architectural and other 'close-range' subjects (see Dallas, 1980a, b), the basic procedure is to take photographs a known base distance apart to provide overlapping coverage of the façade in question, termed *stereo-photography*, and view these in such a way as to reconstruct

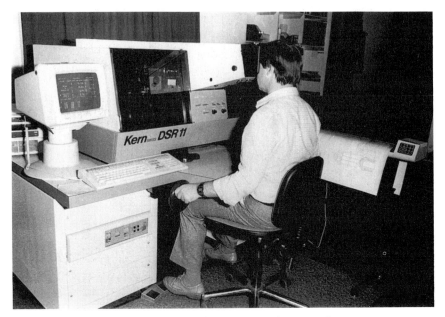

Figure 8.6 Analytical photogrammetric stereo-plotter.

the optical geometry that existed at the time of data capture using an accurate dimensional control framework.

The resulting three-dimensional, mathematical *stereo-model* provides the operator of an analogue, or increasingly used analytical, stereo-plotter with all the information necessary to produce a graphical representation by tracing over the image using a manoeuvrable *measuring mark*, so recording specific features and defining separate planes (Figure 8.6). In this way, plans, sections and elevations may be produced, together with profiles, contours and other physical dimensions (Figure 8.7).

Specialized *metric* cameras are used for photogrammetric recording, possessing certain characteristics which distinguish them from amateur or 'non-metric' cameras, including accurate knowledge of the principal distance and point (perpendicular distance from vertex to image plane and point where perpendicular meets image plane respectively), nominally zero lens distortion and minimal film deformation.

The recent introduction of *partial-metric* cameras has increased both commercial and academic interest in photogrammetry generally, whether in architecture or other disciplines, and, with the new generation of analytical plotters, much can now be achieved with less accurate photographic coverage.

Despite this increase in the use of partial-metric photography, however, it would appear that the more traditional approach will continue to be

Figure 8.7   Photogrammetric plotting table.

relied on by the relatively small number of companies offering this service within the United Kingdom, particularly for complex and large-scale architectural recording, with emphasis placed instead on advances in the methods of image restitution. Increases in microprocessing power have opened up the possibility of deriving data from previously in-compatible sources, and providing digital output for CAD manipulation and enhancement. For a specification of procedures relating particularly to the recording of historic buildings and monuments, see Dallas (1988).

In addition to stereo-photogrammetry as discussed, *orthophotography* offers a little-known method of recording based on photographic data capture, where minute segments of a photograph are re-photographed, but subject to the accuracies of the photogrammetric process. This is achieved by correcting the individual segments when the resulting stereo-model is viewed, and as such the technique is reliant on the use of metric photography and a modified stereo-plotter.

As a practical recording tool, orthophotography favours flat planes, with discontinuances arising at changes in depth due to the failings of either the operator or automated process. Although used more on the Continent, little use has been made of this technique for architectural recording in the United Kingdom.

COMPUTER-AIDED MONO-PHOTOGRAMMETRY

Computer-aided mono-photogrammetry was developed as part of a doctoral research project within the School of the Built Environment, Leicester Polytechnic, as a means of extracting measurements from photographs and restituting the information using computerized draughting facilities (Watt, 1990). Examples of the graphical information produced may be seen in Appendix I.

As the name 'computer-aided mono-photogrammetry' suggests, the data are obtained from a single photographic image, rather than a stereo-pair, using computer-aided draughting or CAD facilities, as a complementary indirect surveying tool for use in producing line drawings of built fabric. In addition, some work has been undertaken on recording from oblique photographs and using archive sources (Watt and Ashton, 1988).

The technique consists in digitizing the required information from an appropriate photograph and correcting this to the desired scale. In practice, therefore, the method of recording can be considered as three separate, though connected, activities: photography, dimensional control and image restitution.

The photography is essentially non-metric and normal to the subject, that is using standard 35 mm equipment to record a façade square-on as described for rectified photography. A shift lens has been widely used, although distortion tests have shown that its use increases the amount of distortion present in the image. As a rule of thumb, only the middle fifty per cent of the image is used to avoid the effects of barrel or pin-cushion distortion, these being lens aberrations that would cause the reproduction of a straight line to appear concave or convex respectively relative to the centre of the image. Black-and-white photography is generally used, with 10 × 8 in. resin-coated, gloss-finished prints found to provide a clear and reasonably stable source from which to work.

Dimensional control is usually based on one horizontal and one vertical measurement taken on the subject façade, using obvious features that are unobstructed on site and so clearly visible on the photograph. If there are obvious projecting and recessed planes to be recorded separately, then separate control is required for each such plane.

Image restitution is based on securing the photographic print to a digitizing tablet of the correct size and resolution, and inputting the image lines as single xy coordinate pairs in order to build up the composition using the particular two-dimensional elements common to the CAD system in use (Figure 8.8).

The digitizing tablet used during the research programme had a resolution of about 350 points per inch (0.07 mm or 0.0028 in.) giving an

Figure 8.8   Digitizing tablet and puck.

accuracy of ±0.254 mm (±0.01 in.) nominal over the active area. Tests on digitizing accuracy using such a tablet showed an average (*x* and *y* axis) accuracy of 0.30 mm (0.12 in.), with a standard deviation of 0.15 mm (0.06 in.). In practice, therefore, dimensional accuracies of ±10–20 mm at a plotting scale of 1 : 50 are possible.

In developing and applying this technique to practical surveying problems found on a variety of building types and sizes, its advantages can be considered to be ease of application, economy both in terms of the equipment used and possibility for in-house application, flexibility of presentation with digital data storage and retrieval, the potential for restituting information from archive sources, and the creation of a photographic archive for immediate or future consumption. Disadvantages include selective practical application, limitations inherent in using simple, small-format photographic equipment, problems of restituting multi-planed and curved façades, and the incidence of errors due to manual digitization.

Further research has been undertaken to assess the viability of scanning graphical information directly from the photographic source, thereby reducing or omitting the need for manual digitization.

At a basic level it is possible to scan a photograhic print to form a raster image or bit map, being made up of a display of pixels, which can then be traced over on screen, thus avoiding the need constantly to refer to a print.

In this way areas of the image can be zoomed in on while tracing, thus increasing the accuracy of the record being produced.

In order for the computer to use scanned data directly, however, it must first receive information in the form of vector coordinates. Whilst it is technically possible to scan in this manner, the costs are prohibitive, and 'pseudo-vectorization', which takes a raster image and converts it into a series of vectors, remains the most realistic option at present, but with limited use for photography-based recording.

REMOTE SENSING

Remote sensing is the general name given to the acquisition and use of data about the earth from sources such as aircraft, balloons, rockets and satellites. Recent developments in sensor and communications technologies, and computing have made possible the effective handling and transfer of data, and rapid processing of imagery.

In the past, the application of such techniques for recording built fabric has been limited to conventional aerial-photographic techniques for archaeological purposes. Recently established science has been employed in the field of architectural analysis and recording to provide clearer and more detailed information relating to construction and decoration. The technique of ground-based remote sensing using 35 mm photography for recording surface and subsurface architectural details is, in particular, helping to form a link between archaeology and architectural analytical survey (Brooke, 1987a,b).

NON-DESTRUCTIVE SURVEYING

Non-destructive surveying includes 'those testing methods for the inspection of buildings (with various degrees of refinement) which do not cause damage to or impair the future life of existing original material so that the architectural, historical and archaeological integrity of the fabric remains unharmed yet analysed' (Fidler, 1980, p. 3).

Whilst recording physical, rather than dimensional, properties, the various methods available allow an insight to be gained into certain aspects of the building fabric, commonly employed in work involving historic buildings and structures. Many of these methods do employ photographic principles relying on the recording of electromagnetic and radiant energy, including radiography, thermography or infra-red detection for condition monitoring, endoscopy, and remote CCTV and video-sensing for surveying drains and other hidden or inaccessible elements of construction. The video camera, in particular, has become a much-used tool for recording background information and the condition of the fabric, and as such can be used to illustrate problems or areas of concern to clients at a later date.

Geophysical sciences have increasingly been applied to identify the presence of underground remains, often in advance of new development. Techniques such as resistivity and proton magnetometry used for this work can be termed *archaeogeophysics*.

Table 8.1   Summary of survey criteria

BUILDING, MONUMENT OR OTHER STRUCTURE		
Architectural heritage	Industrial heritage	Archaeological heritage

PROPOSED WORK	
Dynamic intervention	**Static intervention**
Conservation	Preservation
Rehabilitation	Consolidation
Restoration	Interpretation
Repair	Maintenance

CHARACTERISTICS		
Condition	**Access**	**Scale**
Dangerous	Difficult	Small
Unstable	Limited	Medium
Stable	Scaffolded	Large

FAÇADES				
Single plane	Projections and recesses	Curvature	Ornate detail	Repetitive features

DRAWINGS REQUIRED FOR:				
Listed building consent	Scheduled monument consent	Statutory approval	Interpretative documentation	Archive record

METHODOLOGY		
Direct	Combination	Indirect

SURVEY TO BE CARRIED OUT		
In-house	Bureau services	Consultants

ANALYSIS OF DOCUMENTATION			
Accuracy	Appropriateness	Content	Cost

SUMMARY

Manual or direct surveys, and the preparation of measured drawings, practised widely and generally accepted and understood, remain fundamental to the recording of architectural subjects and their façades. However, as demand ceases to be adequately met by such techniques, and specific requirements necessitate the further use of specialized methods of recording, then the division between direct and indirect forms of survey will broaden.

It is vitally important, however, to see such indirect techniques as useful tools to be employed as conditions dictate, whether as the sole means of recording or reserved for particular parts of a project. They should be seen as being complementary to other forms of recording, and are not to be relied on *per se*: this is particularly true of techniques in their early stages of development.

In order to summarize how architectural photography and related surveying techniques can assist in the practical surveying and recording of buildings, monuments and other structures it is useful to assess their application and performance against certain survey criteria (Table 8.1).

CHAPTER NINE

Modern Survey Methods

INTRODUCTION

The introduction of new technology over the past decade has revolutionized the process of field survey. With current equipment and techniques it is feasible to survey a site without physically measuring, to record site dimensions without completing a fieldbook, and to produce a drawing without touching a scale rule.

Although surveying equipment has become increasingly sophisticated, the reader should not be intimidated. Surveys still require skilled planning but the latest equipment reduces the majority of fieldwork to a button-pushing exercise. Further, the increased capital cost of the systems described can be negated in appropriate circumstances where increased productivity achievable by even a relatively inexperienced user can justify short-term hire.

As with other areas, developments in surveying have resulted from the widening application of information technology. The aim of this chapter is to outline the development and progressive enhancement of techniques and equipment and to describe current survey methodology. It will be observed that such systems have particular relevance to site surveying, but their application to measured building surveys is also covered.

Many of the developments have either occurred concurrently or with significant overlap and, in order to avoid confusion, the chapter addresses chronological developments in each of the following key areas:

Survey techniques
Distance measurement
Angular measurement

Data recording
Reduction and plotting

Following consideration of the above areas, their integration to provide an up-to-date methodology is described.

SURVEY TECHNIQUES

Survey methods described in Chapters 1 and 3 include the following:

Control methods	*Detail methods*
Triangulation	Chaining
Trilateration	Intersection
Traversing	Radial

In seeking to apply information technology (IT) to the survey process it is not necessary to invent new methods, although the introduction of global positioning systems may prove to be a significant exception. Rather, it is a case for examining the characteristics of each method to determine the most suitable.

In a typical site survey there may be over a thousand detail points established from eight stations. Although the accuracy of the control stations is important, sheer weight of numbers forces IT application in the direction of detail survey.

The features offered by IT application should now be considered in order to justify a decision between chaining, intersection and radial methods. General criteria when considering the use of microprocessor-based equipment are as follows:

1. Minimize transportation and setting up of equipment.
2. Generate large quantities of similar data.
3. Facilitate rapid measurement.
4. Maximize reliability of data.
5. Maximize the usefulness of measured data.

Traditional chain survey methods are inappropriate for enhancement due to the dynamic nature of the process. Additionally, in cases where height data are required such information would only result from additional levelling operations.

Intersection can generally be ruled out because of the need for two sets of equipment but does have some merit in special instances of elevational recording as described later.

Fortunately, radial methods satisfy all the above criteria. From a single instrument position it is possible to record any feature that can be observed, subject to the respective accuracy limitations of the available measuring method. By recording three measurements – slope distance, horizontal scale reading and vertical scale reading – a surveyed point can be located in plan and height. Further weight is given to the use of radial techniques in the light of similar measurements being used in providing survey control via traversing.

Having identified radial methods as satisfying the basic criteria, it is appropriate to consider the practical limitations of the method using traditional measuring, booking, and plotting techniques. At its simplest level, a radial survey can be undertaken using a theodolite to measure horizontal and vertical angles, taping the required distances, recording the measurements on an appropriate booking sheet, reducing the data on a calculator to obtain horizontal distance and level, and plotting using a large-diameter protractor. This is the starting point for consideration of the enhancements offered in the following sections.

DISTANCE MEASUREMENT

In the context of detail surveys, although a theodolite can accurately measure angles, manual taping cannot produce commensurate accuracy within an acceptable time scale. At plotting scales larger than 1 : 500, single taped measurements are unlikely to provide sufficient reliability, particularly over uneven surfaces. In order to promote the use of radial techniques it is necessary to seek enhancements in speed and accuracy of distance measurement.

Tacheometry

Speed of measurement can be increased by the use of indirect measuring methods, the original such method being tacheometry.

The most readily available form is stadia tacheometry (described in Chapter 1) where readings onto a vertical staff are multiplied by a constant value to produce a distance measurement. With errors of up to 100 millimetres in any measurement this method cannot safely be used for large-scale surveys except in the context of taking checks to localize gross errors.

Developments in theodolite optics led to the availability of purpose-made tacheometers culminating with the production of self-reducing instruments. Such instruments as the Kern DK-RT enabled a user to sight onto a graduated staff and derive horizontal distance and height difference.

The introduction of such equipment by the Ordnance Survey in the 1950s was justified by improvements in speed, accuracy and cost when compared with traverse and chain methods.

Tacheometers have been superseded in recent years and second-hand outfits are readily available at reasonable prices. However, prospective purchasers of such equipment should be aware of the need for skilled operation and have full knowledge of equipment and methodology. The reader is referred to texts in the bibliography for a detailed description of tacheometric principles and techniques.

Electromagnetic distance measurement (EDM)

During the Second World War the invention of radar established the principle of locating objects using reflected radio waves. Subsequent work carried out by the South African Council for Scientific and Industrial Research, again using radio waves, resulted in the development of equipment suitable for survey application. Known as the Tellurometer, this equipment was accurate but suffered from its bulk and a minimum range of over one hundred metres.

Figure 9.1 EDM detail outfit.

Further research by AGA in Sweden produced the first lightwave-based instrument, the Geodimeter, and set the pattern which has led to today's infra-red EDMs. By incorporating microprocessor technology, manufacturers have achieved significant reductions in size, weight, cost and power supply requirements. In contrast with obtaining tacheometric measurements, EDM provides data following a short measuring cycle and incorporates a liquid crystal display (LCD) for ease of reading. Current EDM technology includes the availability of lightweight instruments to mount on theodolite telescopes, and integration with electronic theodolites to create total stations. Figure 9.1 shows a typical EDM detail outfit.

A typical, low-cost EDM would offer the following performance characteristics:

Weight	0.6 kg
Range (single prism)	800 metres
Range (triple prism)	1200 metres
Standard error	5 mm + 5 p.p.m.
Measuring cycle	5 seconds
Power supply (2 Ah)	1200 measurements

ANGULAR MEASUREMENT

In seeking enhancements in angular measuring technology it should be remembered that the construction and principles of the traditional optomechanical theodolite provide a very effective means of measuring horizontal and vertical angles. However, they do have weaknesses; firstly the wide range of scale reading systems can cause confusion and be time-consuming to use, secondly, and more importantly, in the context of evolving technology, traditional theodolites do not produce digital data.

The solving of the above deficiencies, by replacing the traditional etched glass scales with solid-state electronic devices, has produced the latest generation of digital theodolites showing angular scale readings on liquid crystal displays.

As stated previously, the integration of EDM and digital theodolite technology provides the surveyor with the *total station* – an instrument resembling a theodolite but having extra facilities afforded by EDM and digital displays. A key feature of total stations is their facility to manipulate measured slope distance, using angular data, to produce values for horizontal distances and height differences – all the information required to determine a point's plan position and elevation.

DATA RECORDING

The method of transferring measured data from site to office must be commensurate with the methods used for measuring and plotting. Just as it would be inappropriate to transcribe total station data manually and subsequently retype the information into an office computer, so the use of sophisticated data logging equipment cannot be justified for transferring non-digital data for manual plotting.

If the field equipment, as in the case of a total station, produces digital data then maximum efficiency can only be obtained by ensuring that the data are preserved in this form. This is best achieved by directly downloading the data from the instrument into a storage device known as a data logger. Such devices can take many forms, ranging from the early use of converted pocket calculators, through field-grade portable computers such as the Husky Hunter and Psion Organiser, to dedicated solid-state electronic devices such as Wild's credit-card-sized recording modules.

The key feature of any data logging method is that measured data can easily and accurately be moved from site to office.

REDUCTION AND PLOTTING

Returning from site to the office, the data logger will contain instrument location and orientation information followed by a long list of sets of angular, distance and coding data. These data are easily transferred onto an office computer system. Early computer reduction software would simply take a batch of such data and, by applying and radial to rectangular coordinate transformation, produce an *xyz* coordinate file. This file would be output to a plotting device to generate a points plot to be used as the basis for producing a manually drawn fair plot.

Current computer systems work at a more sophisticated level. Survey control frameworks may be reduced, checked and adjusted using a range of statistically-based methods. Subsequent detail data are orientated and positioned onto the adjusted survey control in both plan and elevation. Depending upon the refinement of the detail coding system, graphical elements (such as line styles and symbols) and text may be generated by the software. The graphical output of modern software packages bears little resemblance to their earlier counterparts as they automatically produce finished plots of very high quality.

COMPUTER-AIDED DESIGN SYSTEMS

Over the recent years there has been a rapid uptake of computer-aided design (CAD) systems by professions associated with development of the built environment. The simplest CAD systems are equivalent to electronic drawing-boards providing facilities for developing and manipulating screen-based drawings which may subsequently be plotted onto a range of media. Manipulating CAD drawings is an efficient process, particularly for applications containing an element of repetition.

At the top end of the CAD market are the sophisticated modelling packages which, in addition to providing a full range of drafting facilities, are capable of producing photo-realistic visualization of proposed developments. Survey data play an important role in such applications by producing an accurate digital terrain model (DTM) of the site.

As site survey data are the basis for many development schemes, it is understandable that as the use of CAD has grown, so have the demands for compatible site survey data. There are few things more frustrating for a CAD user than having to digitize site survey data from a paper plot. It would seem obvious that if the surveyor is using a computer system to produce a survey plot then the data file could easily be transferred to, say, an architect's CAD system. Sadly, this is not necessarily the case as different computer systems tend to use different structures for the data. Inevitably, the data can only be transferred by converting to a neutral file format, such as IGES or DXF, which the target system can read.

Whatever the transfer method, CAD systems place extra demands on the survey process because they work at a scale of 1:1. This contrasts sharply with the latitude available when plotting at a scale of 1:500 where the smallest plottable distance is generally accepted as 100 millimetres. Viewed optimistically, CAD provides an opportunity to maintain the accuracy of the survey throughout the construction process.

BUILDING SURVEYS

With radical changes having been made to the site survey process, it is appropriate to consider similar developments emerging in the recording of building plans, sections and elevations.

The modern armoury of surveying equipment and computer processing technology provides the opportunity to solve complex recording problems. If there is a trigonometrical solution then a combination of surveying hardware and computer software can be formulated. However, such specialized applications lie outside the bounds of this text and consideration will be restricted to areas where survey methods have been significantly improved by incorporating new technology.

As stated earlier, instrument-based methods are most successful where large numbers of similar data can be recorded from a single position. This is rarely the case in measured building surveys. The most notable contribution of new instrumentation has been the use of total station and data logging equipment in recording irregularly shaped floor plans. Using a total station in conjunction with a small prism it is possible to define the plan geometry of spaces bounded by splayed or curved walls far more accurately than is possible using any other method.

Indirect measurement methods such as sonic tapes have found some acceptance, but the inaccuracy of current models restricts their use in measured surveys. More promising is the recent availability of hand-held EDMs which do not require prisms to reflect their infra-red beam. This equipment offers accuracy similar to its instrument-based counterpart and could be particularly appropriate for, say, recording running dimensions along corridors and on external façades.

Attempts have been made to introduce data logging methods in recording measured survey data. There are significant problems of developing software sufficiently flexible to deal with all features encountered in buildings. Of note is the Pyramid Plus system which is based on a Psion Organiser and has proved extremely effective in recording floor plans, although it should be pointed out that an AutoCAD workstation is needed to process the data.

Practitioners have been slow to adopt CAD systems for use in recording buildings. Whilst it is true that CAD is particularly productive in the context of building design, it also offers features which will broaden its appeal.

Hand Signals

Figure A1   Hand signals.

Common Abbreviations

Aggregate	agg
Air admittance valve	AAV
Airbrick	AB
Airing cupboard	AC
Aluminium	al
As before described	a.b.d.
Artificial	art
Asbestos cement	a.c.
Asphalt	asph
Back inlet gulley	BIG
Basement	bsmt
Bath	Ba
Bearers	brrs
Bitumen	bit
Blockwork	blkwk
Boarding	bdg
Boiler	b
Both sides	b.s.
Bottom	btm
Brackets	brkts
Breaking joint	b.j.
Brick (as a measurement of thickness)	B; ½B = 112 mm; 1B = 225 mm
Brick-on-edge	b.o.e.
Brickwork	bkk
Built in	b.i.
Cantilever	cantl

Cast iron	c.i.
Cavity	cav
Ceiling	clg
Cement	ct
Cement : lime : sand	c.l.s.
Central heating	CH
Centre line	c.l.
Centre-to-centre	c/c
Chromium plate	CP
Circular	circ
Circular on plan	c on p
Close copper nailing	c.c.n.
Cold water service	CWS
Cold water storage tank	CWST
Common brickwork	c.b
Concrete	conc
Coping	cpg
Copper	Cu
Corrugated asbestos cement	c.a.c.
Corrugated galvanized iron	c.g.i.
Countersunk	csk
Course	cos
Cupboard	cpbd
Cylinder	cyl
Damp-proof course	d.p.c.
Damp-proof membrane	d.p.m.
Deep	dp
Diameter	dia
Drain	dr
Earthenware	e'ware
Existing	extg
External	ext
Fair faced	f.f.
Finished floor level	FFL
Fire hydrant	FH
Floor	flr
Foundation	fndn
Framed ledged and braced	f.l. & b.
Fresh air inlet	FAI
Galvanized	galv
Galvanized iron	g.i.
Glazed vitrified clay	GVC
Grease trap	GT

Ground floor	GF
Ground level	GL
Gulley	G
Half round	HR
Hardwood	h.w.
Header tank	H.T.
Height	ht
Herringbone strutting	h.b.s.
Horizontal	horiz
Hot water service	HWS
Housed	hsd
Inspection chamber	IC
Insulation	insul
Intercepting trap	IT
Invert	inv
Joint	jnt
Joist	jst
Junction	junc
Lath and plaster	l & p
Lead	Pb
Left hand	LH
Length	l
Lime and hair	l & h
Manhole	MH
Mild steel	MS
Moulded	mld
Mullion	mull
Not to scale	NTS
Number	No.
One side only	o.s.o.
Open top	OT
Ordnance Survey bench-mark	OSBM
Overall	o/a
Overflow	o'flow
Overhang	o'hang
Oversailing	o'slg
Pair	pr
Parapet	ppt
Partition	ptn
Petrol interceptor	PI
Plain edged	p.e.
Plaster	plstr
Plaster-board	p.b.

Polished brass	PB
Polyvinyl chloride	p.v.c.
Post and rail	p + r
Post and wire	p + w
Quarry tile	q.t.
Radiator	rad
Rail	rl
Rainwater head	RWH
Rainwater outlet	RWO
Rainwater pipe	RWP
Rebate	reb
Reinforced concrete	RC
Right hand	RH
Rising main	RM
Rodding eye	RE
Salt glazed	s.g.
Septic tank	ST
Sink	S
Skirting	sktg
Soffit	soff
Softwood	s.w.
Soil and vent pipe	SVP
Soil pipe	SP
Square	sq
Stainless steel	s.s.
Stop tap pit	STP
Stop valve	SV
Temporary bench-mark	TBM
Terra-cotta	TC
Thick	th
Tongued and grooved	t & g
Underside	u/s
Urinal	U
Vent pipe	VP
Vertical	vert
Wash hand basin	WHB
Waste pipe	WP
Water closet	WC

Setting Out for Common Arch Shapes

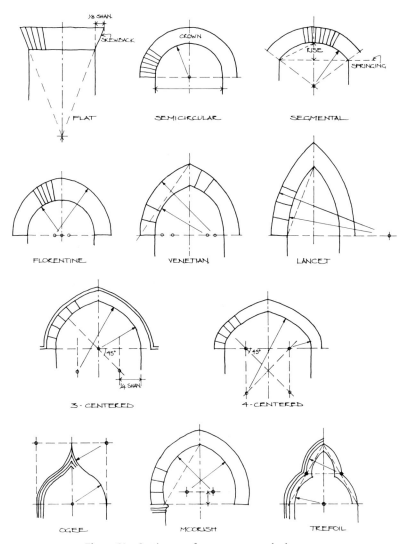

Figure C1 Setting out for common arch shapes.

Common Mouldings

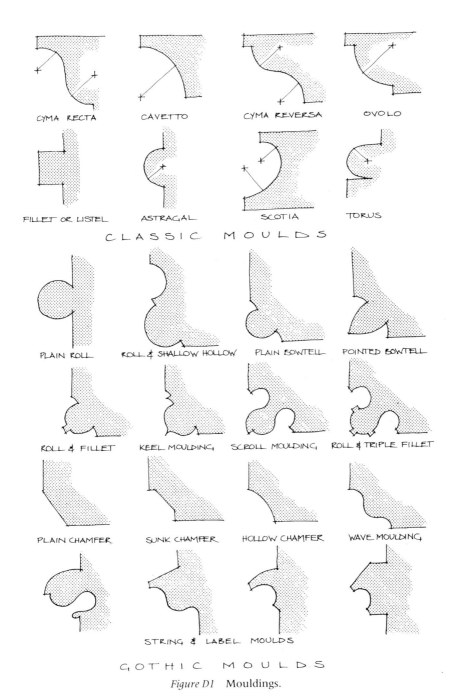

Figure D1 Mouldings.

Practical Examples: Using Rod and Tape

The following drawings and field-notes were prepared by part-time M.A. students in Architectural Building Conservation at De Montfort University, as part of their first-year coursework programme. The surveys were carried out using a surveyor's rod and tape only.

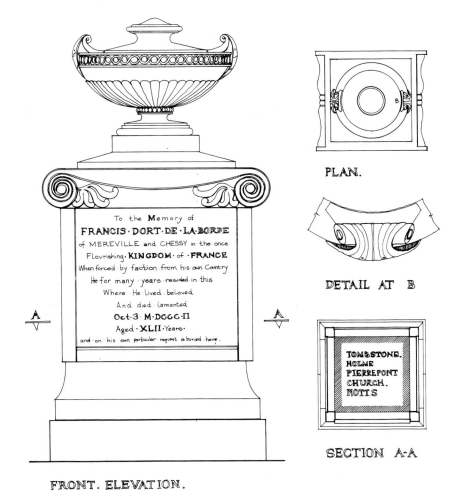

PLAN.

DETAIL AT B

SECTION A-A

FRONT. ELEVATION.

Figure E1 Part of a survey drawing of a funerary monument at Holme Pierrepont Church, Nottinghamshire. Reproduced by kind permission of the surveyor, Bruce Bradley.

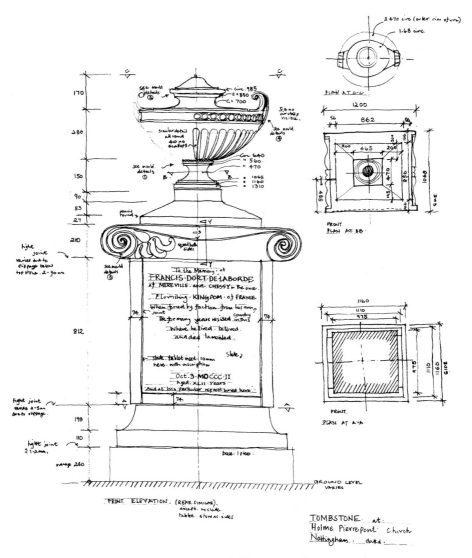

Figure E2 An extract from the survey field-notes used to prepare the survey drawing of a funerary monument at Holme Pierrepont Church, Nottinghamshire (Figure E1). Reproduced by kind permission of the surveyor, Bruce Bradley.

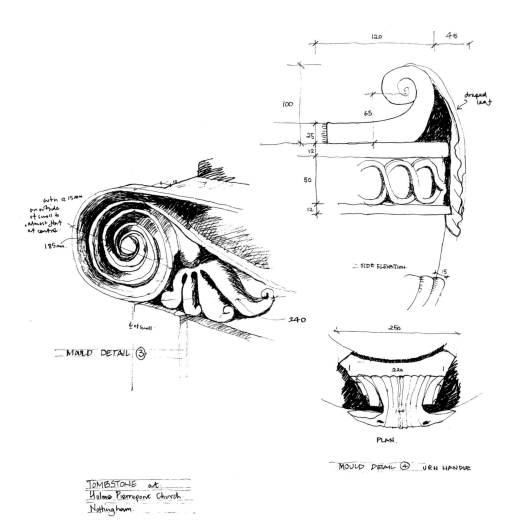

120   46

100

65

25

12

50

12

draped leaf

SIDE ELEVATION.

15

extn ≈ 15mm on outside of scroll to almost start at centre

185mm.

₵ of scroll

140

MOULD DETAIL ③

250

226

140

PLAN.

MOULD DETAIL ④   URN HANDLE

TOMBSTONE at Holme Pierrepont Church Nottingham

Figure E3   An extract from the survey field-notes used to prepare the survey drawing of a funerary monument at Holme Pierrepont Church, Nottinghamshire (Figure E1). Reproduced by kind permission of the surveyor, Bruce Bradley.

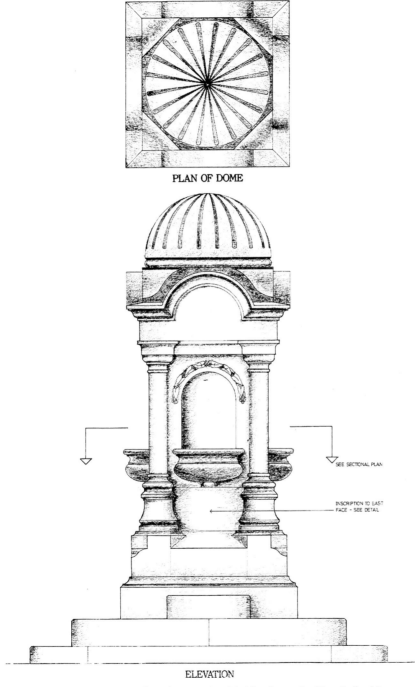

PLAN OF DOME

SEE SECTIONAL PLAN

INSCRIPTION TO EAST
FACE - SEE DETAIL

ELEVATION

Figure E4 Elevation and plan of a Victorian drinking fountain, New Oxford Street, London. Reproduced by kind permission of the surveyor, Hilary Brightman.

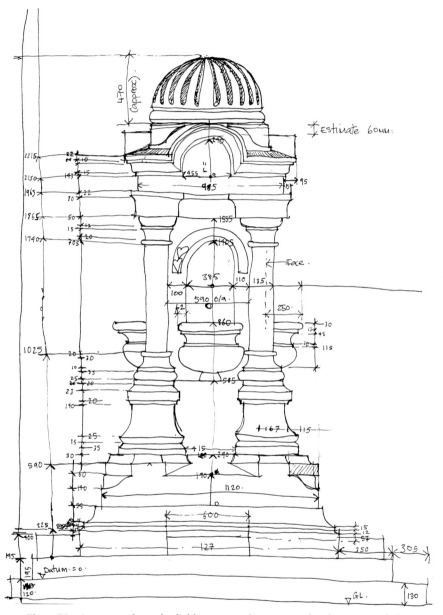

Figure E5   An extract from the field-notes used to prepare the elevation and plan of a Victorian drinking fountain, New Oxford Street, London (Figure E4). Reproduced by kind permission of the surveyor, Hilary Brightman.

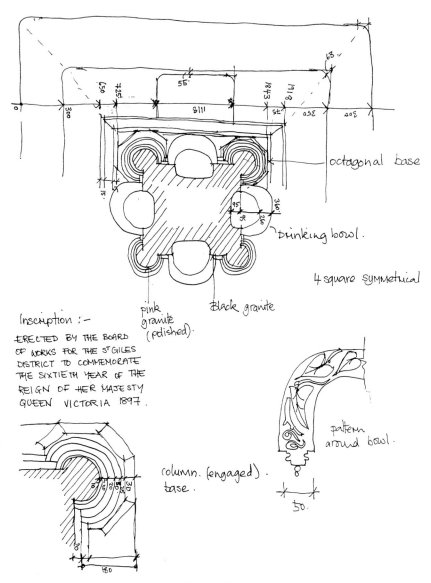

octagonal base

drinking bowl.

4 square symmetrical

Black granite

pink
granite
(polished).

Inscription :-

ERECTED BY THE BOARD
OF WORKS FOR THE St GILES
DISTRICT TO COMMEMORATE
THE SIXTIETH YEAR OF THE
REIGN OF HER MAJESTY
QUEEN VICTORIA 1897.

pattern
around bowl.

column. (engaged).
base.

Figure E5   continued

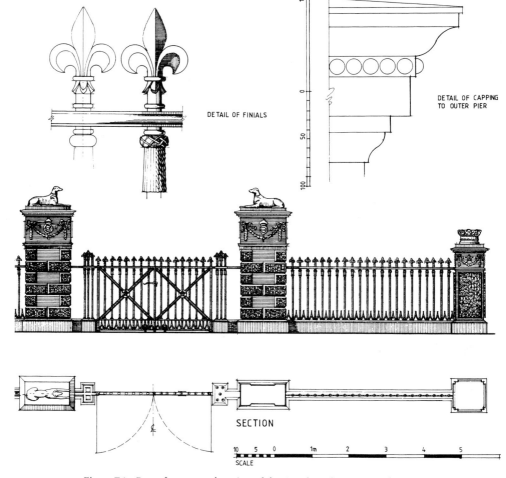

Figure E6 Part of a survey drawing of the South Lodge gates and piers at Clumber Park, Nottinghamshire. Reproduced by kind permission of the surveyor, Denise Sweeney.

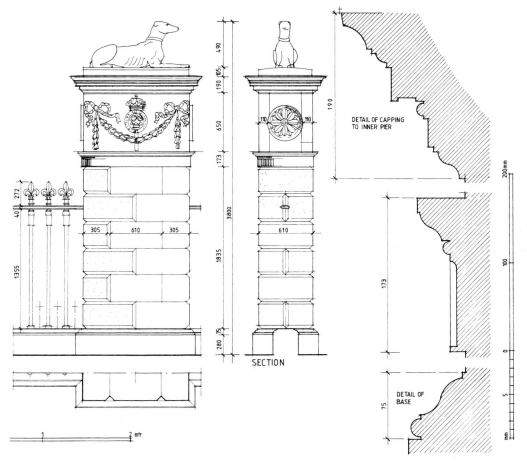

Figure E7 Part of a survey drawing showing details of the gate piers at South Lodge, Clumber Park, Nottinghamshire. Reproduced by kind permission of the surveyor, Denise Sweeney.

Practical Example: Plotting on the Spot

This survey of Long Melford church, Suffolk, was measured and drawn on the spot to a scale of a quarter of an inch to a foot by the Leicester architect Walter Brand in 1894. This technique has the advantage that the finished drawing may be checked against the building for accuracy before leaving the site.

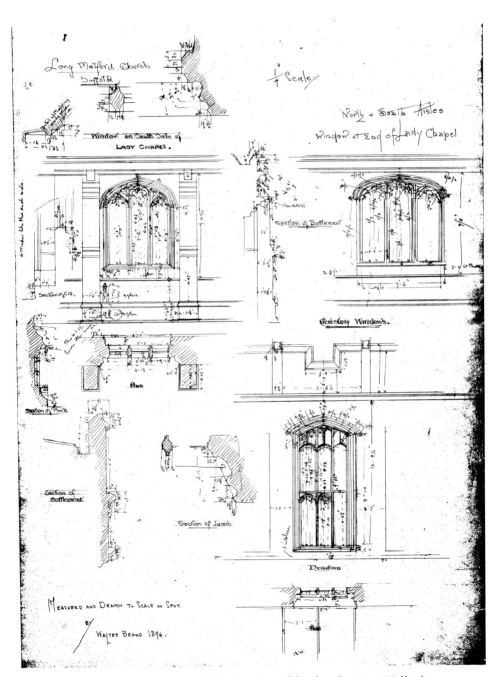

Figure F1 Part of a survey of the elevations of the church at Long Melford, Suffolk, plotted on the spot by Walter Brand in 1894.

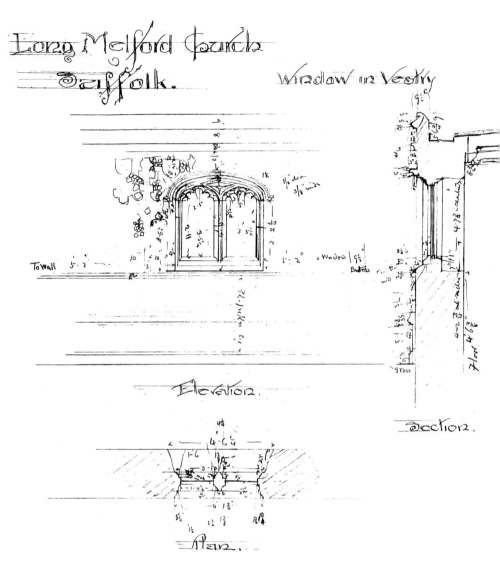

Figure F2   An extract from a detailed measured survey of a window at Long
Melford church, Suffolk, plotted on the spot by Walter Brand in 1894.

Practical Examples: Recording Domestic Vernacular Buildings

The drawings of King's Head Cottage, Banham, Norfolk, show respectively: a ground floor plan, longitudinal section and a metric projection of a timber-framed house. The surveyor, Robert Smith, is a specialist in interpreting timber-framed buildings and, rather than sketching and recording measurements on site for plotting later in the office, he prefers to produce an accurate scale drawing on site using pencil, scale rule and compasses which is later traced off in the office to produce the final survey drawing. By using this method Mr Smith never has any worries about missing anything, all relevant detail is picked up as he looks carefully at the built fabric for evidence of its construction, for example peg holes, mortices and so on, and everything is drawn on an A4 clipboard. Although no dimensions are booked down using this method, it has much to offer when recording and interpreting the construction of a timber-framed building.

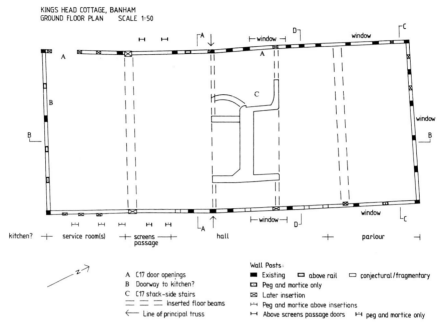

KINGS HEAD COTTAGE, BANHAM
GROUND FLOOR PLAN   SCALE 1:50

kitchen?   service room(s)   screens   hall   parlour
passage

A C17 door openings
B Doorway to kitchen?
C C17 stack-side stairs
— — — Inserted floor beams
← Line of principal truss

Wall Posts:
■ Existing   ▭ above rail   ▢ conjectural/fragmentary
▢ Peg and mortice only
⊠ Later insertion
⊢⊣ Peg and mortice above insertions
⊢⊣ Above screens passage doors   ⊢⊣ peg and mortice only

Figure G1   Ground floor plan of King's Head Cottage, Banham, Norfolk.
Reproduced by kind permission of Robert Smith/Norfolk County Council.

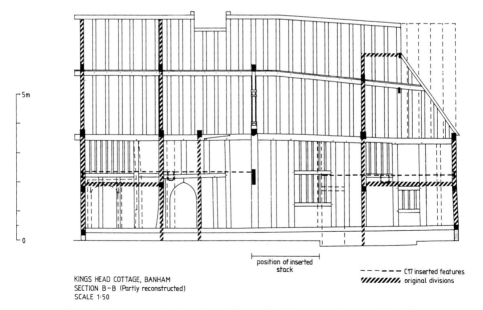

position of inserted
stack

KINGS HEAD COTTAGE, BANHAM
SECTION B–B (Partly reconstructed)
SCALE 1:50

– – – – – C17 inserted features
▨▨▨ original divisions

Figure G2   Longitudinal section of King's Head Cottage, Banham, Norfolk.
Reproduced by kind permission of Robert Smith-Norfolk County Council.

King's Head Cottage
Banham

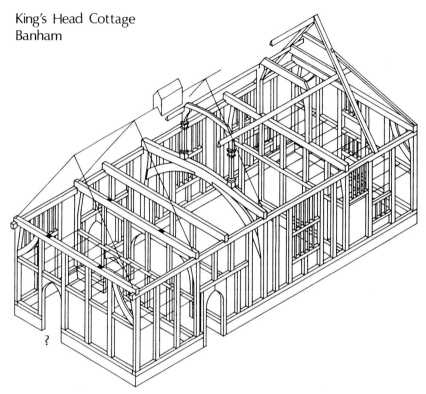

Figure G3   Metric projection of King's Head Cottage, Banham, Norfolk.
Reproduced by kind permission of Robert Smith/Norfolk County Council.

Practical Examples: Industrial Archaeological/ Vernacular Recording

A standardized approach to the recording of information on a particular building type, in this instance a dovecote at Morton-cum-Fiskerton, Nottinghamshire, is illustrated. For each building, information on the building and its construction is collected in written form on standard pro forma to supplement the information contained on a measured survey drawing.

Figures H5 and H6 show survey notes recording a dovecote at Bleasby, Nottinghamshire.

DOVECOTE SURVEY

Address _Morton Manor Farm. Morton-cum-Fiskerton. Newark Notts._

OS Map Ref (1:50 000) _120   725 514_   Date _Feb 1988_   Surveyor _J.A. SEVERN._

Local authority area _NEWARK and SHERWOOD DISTRICT COUNCIL_

Hints on location _Can be seen across railway from Road from Southwell_

A. GENERAL

1. Name and address of owner — _MR Robert Hammond. Messrs J. Hammond & Co Morton Manor Farm. Morton Southwell Notts NG25 0UK_

2. Name and address of tenant — _Not Applicable._

3. Position of cote in relation to main building — _Stands away from Farmhouse across the garden to the North adjacent to farmyard._

4. Situation of cote (ground level, a hill, mound of high ground, etc.) — _At ground level near a stream._

5. Type of estate (ecclesiastical, manorial, etc.) — _Manorial._

B. STRUCTURE

6. Structure type (independent or composite) — _Independant and still free standing_

7. If composite – no. of storeys and which contains the cote — _Not Applicable._

8. Construction materials (stone, brick, timber, etc., or combination) — _Base of stone. brick walls and timber corner posts._

9. If brick, description and size — _Red: handmade: 4c/s=10½". size 9½"x4½"x2"._

10. Shape (square, octagonal, etc.) — _Square._

11. Type of floor (stone, brick, puddled clay, tile, etc.) — _New concrete._

12. Shape of roof (hipped, gabled, etc.) — _Pyramid._

13. Roof covering (stone flags, slates, red tile, grey slate, wood shingles, etc.) — _Red clay handmade plain tiles._

14. Position and description of glover(s) — _at top of pyramid._

15. Other roof termination and finial (gabled, louvred, etc.) and whether surmounted by weathervane, etc. —

16. Position and description of flight holes — _only remaining were in glover (but see Whitaker)_

17. External measurements of building — _17'-4" x 17'-2½"_

18. Internal measurements or thickness — _walls only half brick thick (see plan)_

19. Does the building bear a date, or any incised inscription, coat of arms, etc.; if so, in what form? — _No._

20. Approximate date of construction — _late 17th century say 1680_

21. Is the work original or much restored? — _most original. but has an inserted floor._

22. Is the cote in good repair or ruinous? — _recently repaired by Tuck's Southwell._

23. Is the building in any danger of demolition? — _No._

Figure H1   Part of a survey pro forma recording details of a dovecote at Morton-cum-Fiskerton, Nottinghamshire. Reproduced by kind permission of John Severn, Severn Stewart Architects, Nottingham.

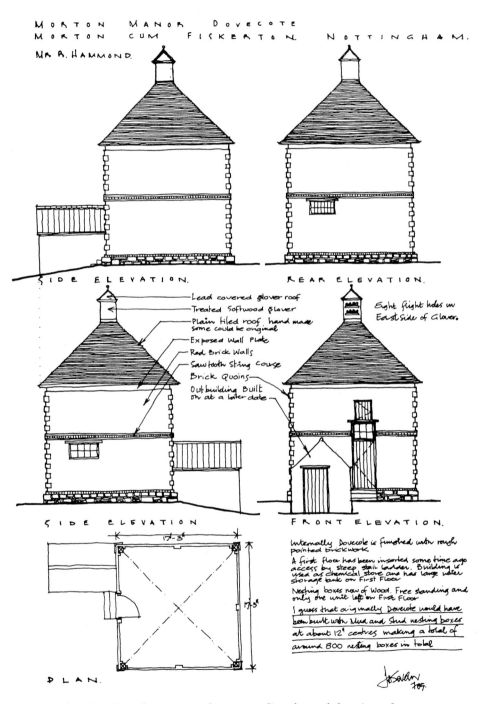

Figure H2 Part of a survey pro forma recording plan and elevations of a dovecote at Morton-cum-Fiskerton, Nottinghamshire. Reproduced by kind permission of John Severn, Severn Stewart Architects, Nottingham.

24. If ruinous, how much of the structure survives?

24. *Not Applicable.*

25. Is building scheduled as an Ancient Monument?

25. *No.*

26. Is building listed under Town and Country Planning Acts?

26. *Listed Grade II.*

C. NESTING ARRANGMENTS

27. Number of tiers of nests

27. *Separate wooden nesting boxes in banks*

28. Number of nests in each tier (excluding gable walls)

28. *Numbers not known (see Whitaker)*

29. Number of nests in each gable wall

29. *Not known*

30. Total number of nests

30. *Not known*

31. Material (brick, stone, wood, tile, or puddled clay)

31. *Separate boxes in wood made up in banks*

32. Is cote still used by pigeons?

32. *No used as a chemical store.*

33. Shape of nests

33. *rectangular*

34. Approximate measurements of nest, i.e., 18" deep

34. *about 12" deep if that.*

35. Are nests grouped on all sides of cote?

35. *Assumed nesting boxes all round.*

36. Is there an alighting board or ledge for pigeons; if so, how many tiers and nests to each alighting board?

36. *Not applicable*

37. Any evidence of a potence being installed?

37. *No.*

38. Is there an alighting board to potence?

38. *Not Applicable.*

39. How did birds enter the cote, if not by a glover (holes cut in gable end, etc.)?

39. *via central glover (see Whitaker).*

40. Doors and windows — where situated and at what level?

40. *Door on East wall with pitching door over. One window on South and West on ground floor*

41. Any protection revealed on the structure to prevent vermin entering cote?

41. *Decorative Rat Ledge stretcher. sawtooth. header.*

D. MISCELLANEOUS

42. By what name is the building commonly known, i.e., Pigeon house, Pigeon tower, duffus, dove house, dovecote, etc.?

42. *Dovecote.*

43. Present usage (if not housing pigeons)?

43. *chemical store for farm.*

44. Any feature peculiar to this dovecote?

44. *yes brick quoins and post construction*

45. Has dovecote to your knowledge been described in any publication? If so, give precise reference

45. *yes Whitaker 1927 "medieval dovecotes in Nottinghamshire"*

46. Are current photographs and/or drawings available?

46. *yes coloured prints and slides by J.A.Severn.*

47. Is there a plan available?

47. *yes attached.*

48. Is there any story or legend associated with the dovecote?

48. *None Known.*

Figure H3 Part of a survey pro forma recording details of a dovecote at Morton-cum-Fiskerton, Nottinghamshire. Reproduced by kind permission of John Severn, Severn Stewart Architects, Nottingham.

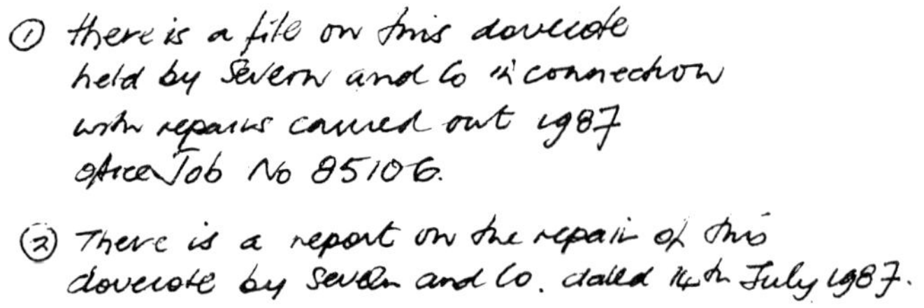

① there is a file on this dovecote
held by Severn and Co in connection
with repairs carried out 1987
Architect Job No 85106.

② There is a report on the repair of this
dovecote by Severn and Co. dated 14th July 1987.

Figure H4 Part of a survey pro forma recording details of a dovecote at Morton-cum-Fiskerton, Nottinghamshire. Reproduced by kind permission of John Severn, Severn Stewart Architects, Nottingham.

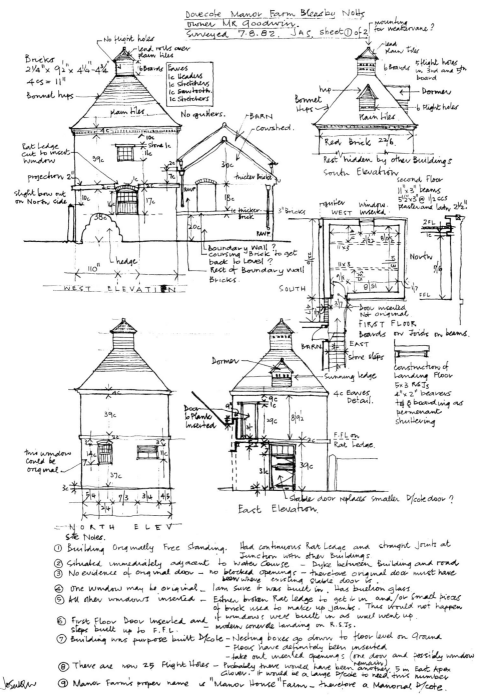

Figure H5 Part of the survey field-notes recording the elevations of a dovecote at Bleasby, Nottinghamshire. Reproduced by kind permission of John Severn, Severn Stewart Architects, Nottingham.

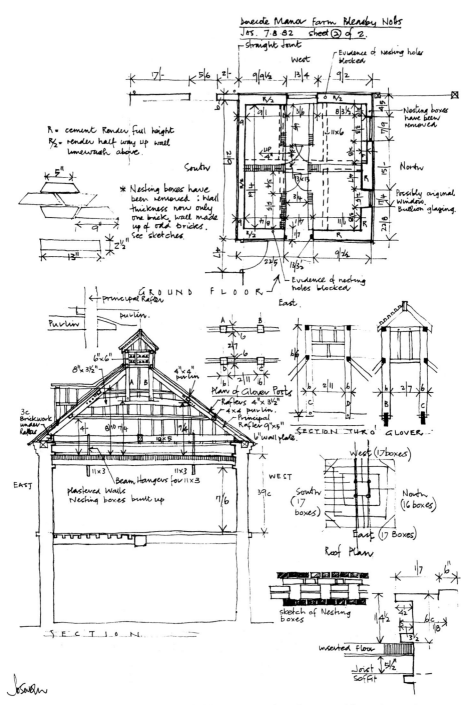

Figure H6 Part of the survey field-notes recording the ground floor plan and cross-section of a dovecote at Bleasby, Nottinghamshire. Reproduced by kind permission of John Severn, Severn Stewart Architects, Nottingham.

Practical Examples: Computer-aided Mono-photogrammetry

The drawings in this appendix were created using the computer-aided mono-photogrammetry technique developed by David Watt and described in Chapter 8.

The survey of King's Mill Viaduct, Mansfield, Nottinghamshire (Figure I1) was commissioned to record both the upstream and downstream faces of this important pre-locomotive viaduct, constructed in 1817, and illustrates all stones, pattress plates and areas of distress. The completed survey was used not only to provide an archive record appropriate to the status of the structure as a scheduled ancient monument but also as part of the contract documentation for a programme of repair works.

Figure I1 King's Mill Viaduct, Mansfield, Nottinghamshire. Reproduced by kind permission of David Watt/Derek Latham and Company, Architects, Derby.

Figure 12 Hales Street Grammar School (west elevation), Coventry, Warwickshire. Reproduced by kind permission of David Watt/S.A. Wright, Architects, Coventry.

The subject building of Figure 12 – Hales Street Grammar School, Coventry, Warwickshire – represents the only remains of a hospital founded in the twelfth century, to which additions have been made in the late nineteenth and early twentieth centuries. This survey was commissioned to produce a set of elevational drawings, showing individual stones and details, suitable for communicating the nature and extent of stonework replacement and repairs, and fulfilling the condition for recording placed in the Schedule Monument Consent granted for this work.

The survey of 'Flacketts', Flacketts Lane, Sudbury, Derbyshire (Figure 13), a timber-framed structure dating from the late sixteenth century, was undertaken to provide a comparison, both in terms of procedure and product, with conventional manual measurement and drawing, as undertaken by an archaeologist producing a series of drawings as part of an interpretive study. The results of the study demonstrated that even for small, apparently simple façades, there are benefits to be gained from using computer-aided mono-photogrammetry, in terms of accuracy and content.

The importance of recording aspects of townscape and urban fabric is rapidly increasing as the infrastructure of settlements is being changed to meet the demands of modern lifestyles and businesses. The survey of the market-place, Aylsham, Norfolk (Figure 14) was undertaken to determine the relative merits of computer-aided mono-photogrammetry as a method for recording a range of building frontages with varied fenestration patterns, doorcases and surface details as represented by this group of eighteenth and nineteenth century buildings on the west side of the market-place in Aylsham. The results of this study demonstrated that a

Figure 13   'Flacketts', Flacketts Lane, Sudbury, Derbyshire. Reproduced by kind permission of David Watt/Derek Latham and Company, Architects, Derby.

series of building façades could be economically recorded using this technique (computer-aided mono-photogrammetry), where the intention is to provide a graphical record as an end in itself, or as a tool for the implementation of a visual impact analysis. Mr R. Dallas, Chief Surveyor for the English Heritage Photogrammetric Unit, York, considers that computer-aided mono-photogrammetry provides a useful technique for this type of work where a precise full photogrammetric survey would be inappropriate both in terms of cost and the accuracy required.

Figure 14   The market-place, Aylsham, Norfolk. Reproduced by kind permission of David Watt.

Bibliography

Bodey, H. and Hallas, M. (1978) *Elementary Surveying for Industrial Archaeologists*. Aylesbury: Shire Publications.

Bracegirdle, B. (1971) 'Photography for industrial archaeology', in Cossons, N. and Hudson, K. (eds), *Industrial Archaeologists Guide 1971–73*. Newton Abbot: David & Charles, pp. 157–71.

Brandon, R. and Brandon, J. A. (1874) *Analysis of Gothick Architecture*, 2nd edn. London.

British Standards Institution (BSI) *BS 1192 Construction Drawing Practice*. London: BSI.

    (1984) Part 1 *Recommendations for general principles*.

    (1987) Part 2 *Recommendations for architectural and engineering drawings*.

    (1987) Part 3 *Recommendations for symbols and other graphic conventions*.

    (1984) Part 4 *Recommendations for landscape drawings*.

    (1990) Part 5 *Guide for the structuring of computer graphic information*.

British Standards Institution (BSI) (1980) *BS 5964 Methods for Setting Out and Measurement of Buildings*. London: BSI.

British Standards Institution (BSI) (1988) *BS 6953 Terms for Procedures for Setting Out, Measurement and Surveying Buildings*. London: BSI.

Brooke, C. J. (1987a) 'Ground-based remote sensing and methods of archaeological information recovery with special reference to churches in the East Midlands', 2 vols. PhD thesis, Dept of Archaeology, University of Nottingham.

Brooke, C. J. (1987b) 'Ground-based remote sensing for archaeological information recovery in historic buildings', *International Journal of Remote Sensing*, 8(7): 1039–48.

Buchanan, T. (1983) *Photographing Historic Buildings for the Record*. London: HMSO.

Chitham, R. (1991) *Measured Drawings for Architects*. London: Butterworth Architecture.

Cocke, T., Findlay, P., Halsey, R. and Williamson, E. (1982) *Recording a Church*. London: Council for British Archaeology.

Cooper, N. (1982) 'The Royal Commission on the Historical Monuments (England) and the National Monuments Record', Report from Seminar on the Recording of Buildings, 31 March 1982, *Transactions of the Association for Studies in the Conservation of Historic Buildings*, 7: 11–13.

Cooper, N. (1988a) 'Architects and historians: recording historic buildings', *Transactions of the Association for Studies in the Conservation of Historic Buildings*, 13: 42–5.

Cooper, N. (1988b) 'The recording of threatened buildings: an aspect of the work of the Royal Commission on the Historical Monuments of England', *Transactions of the Ancient Monuments Society*, 35: 28–45.

Council for British Archaeology (CBA) (1985) *Halleluiah. Recording Chapels and Meeting Houses*. London: CBA.

Curl, J. S. (1992) *Encyclopaedia of Architectural Terms*. London: Donhead.

Dallas, R. W. A. (1980a) 'Architectural and archaeological recording', in Atkinson, K. B. (ed.), *Developments in Close-range Photogrammetry. 1.* Barking: Applied Science Publishers, pp. 81–116.

Dallas, R. W. A. (1980b) 'Surveying with a camera: photogrammetry', *Architects' Journal*, 171(5): 249–55.

Dallas, R. W. A. (1980c) 'Surveying with a camera: rectified photography', *Architects' Journal*, 171(8): 395–99.

Dallas, R. W. A. (1988) *A Specification for the Architectural Photogrammetric Survey of Historic Buildings and Monuments*. Kyoto, Japan: International Society for Photogrammetry and Remote Sensing (ISPRS), Archives Commission V.

Dallas, R. W. A. (1991) 'The land surveyor's contribution to the surveying and recording of historic monuments, buildings and landscapes'. Paper presented at Surveying and Mapping '89, *Proceedings of the 3rd National Land Surveying and Mapping Conference and Exhibition*, Institution and College Conference, University of Warwick, 17–21 April, Session D, paper D4, 1–12.

Dirsztay, P. (1989) *Inside Churches: A Guide to Church Furnishings*. London: National Association of Decorative and Fine Arts Society.

Earl, J. (1982) 'Measured drawing: 'The Survey of London' tradition, *Transactions of the Association for Studies in the Conservation of Historic Buildings*, 7: 19–26.

Fidler, J. (1980) 'Non-destructive surveying techniques for the analysis of historic buildings', *Transactions of the Association for Studies in the Conservation of Historic Buildings*, 5: 3–10.

Forrester, H. (1972) *Mediaeval Gothic Mouldings*. Chichester: Phillimore.

Harwood, T. (1982) *A Guide to Surveying Techniques*. London: Northwood.

Hedgecoe, J. (1977) *The Photographer's Handbook.* London: Ebury.

Hum-Hartley, S. (1978) 'Non-destructive testing for heritage structures', *Association for Preservation Technology Bulletin*, X(3): 4–20.

International Council on Monuments and Sites (ICOMOS) (1990) *Guide to Recording Historic Buildings*. London: Butterworth Architecture.

Jones, J. (1984) *How to Record Graveyards*, 3rd edn. London: Council for British Archaeology.

Kerr, J. (1989) 'Archaeological recording of historic buildings', *English Heritage Conservation Bulletin*, 7 (February): 7–9.

Lewis, P. and Darley, G. (1986) *Dictionary of Ornament*. London: Macmillan.

McDowall, R. W. (1980) *Recording Old Houses: A Guide*. London: Council for British Archaeology.

Noble, G. (1982) 'The role of photographic archives in conservation', *Transactions of the Association for Studies in the Conservation of Historic Buildings*, 7: 27–41.

Reekie, F. (1976) *Draughtsmanship: Architectural and Building Graphics*. London: Edward Arnold.

Royal Commission on the Historical Monuments of England (RCHME) (1991) *Recording Historic Building: A Descriptive Specification*, 2nd edn. London: RCHME.

Royal Commission on the Historical Monuments of England/Society of Architectural Historians of Great Britain (RCHME/SAHGB) (1991) *Recording Historic Buildings. Papers from symposium held on 11 May 1991 at the Architectural Association, London*. London: RCHME.

Royal Institution of Chartered Surveyors (RICS) (1991) *Surveying Safely: A Personal Commitment*. London: RICS.

Smith, L. (1985) *Investigating Old Buildings*. London: Batsford.

Watt, D. S. (1990) *The Development and Application of Computer-Aided Mono-Photogrammetry for Recording Architectural Façades*, 2 vols. PhD thesis, School of the Built Environment, Leicester Polytechnic.

Watt, D. S. and Ashton, R. G. (1988) 'An ancient cellar: where new meets old. A demonstration of computer-aided mono-photogrammetry', *Transactions of the Association for Studies in the Conservation of Historic Buildings*, 13: 9–14.

Whyte, W. S. and Paul, R. (1985) *Basic Metric Surveying*, 3rd edn. London: Butterworth.

Wills, C. and Wills, D. (1980) *History of Photography: Techniques and Equipment*. London: Hamlyn.

Index